SAVE 10% on *Science Magnifier*™ Desk Copy 1st Printing

This offer applies only to the purchase of the Desk Copy 1st Printing edition of *Science Magnifier*™ and is good while supplies last. Include promotion code **FS** with your phone, fax, or mail order; for an online order, type **FS** in the Promotion Code box during checkout. Offer cannot be combined with any other offer or contract pricing; cannot be used to purchase STC Program™, Math Out of the Box®, Building Blocks of Science®, or GEMS® materials; and cannot be used to credit your account.

Carolina Biological Supply Company
2700 York Rd • Burlington NC 27215-3398
Call: 800.334.5551 • Fax: 800.222.7112 • Online: www.carolina.com

www.carolinacurriculum.com

Published by Carolina Biological Supply Company

Send all inquiries to:
Carolina Biological Supply Company
Curriculum Division
2700 York Road
Burlington, NC 27215-3387

ISBN-13: 978-1-4350-0590-7

First printing.
Printed in the United States of America.

Reviewers

Dr. Michael Klentschy
San Diego, CA

Ron DeFronzo
Warren, RI

Tom Peters
Clemson, SC

Dr. Sandy Ledwell, NBCT
Montgomery, AL

Juanita Juárez, English Language Learners Consultant
Austin, TX

Development Team

Cindy Morgan, Director, Product and Development,
Carolina Curriculum, a Division of Carolina Biological
Supply Company

Marsha W. Jones, Developer,
Carolina Curriculum, a Division of Carolina Biological
Supply Company

Dr. Donovan Leonard
Appalachian State University
Boone, NC

Contents

Science Basics

Life Science

Earth Science

Physical Science

Study Guide

Will loves skateboarding and other sports. His favorite science is physical science. He is very curious!

Marty the Meerkat is the mascot for the Science Magnifiers. He came from the Kalahari Desert in southern Africa. Marty might pop up anywhere!

Rain really likes Earth science, too. She wants to tell everyone about recycling. Her dog, **Rocket**, helps her out.

Tomás likes to go rock climbing. When he isn't climbing, he studies rocks. He loves Earth science.

Appendices

Chase loves to read about life science. He also works on his computer and is building his robot, Kelvin.

Kari goes to karate class after school. She likes physical science. She carries a science notebook just about everywhere.

Mai is a nice young lady. She loves to dance. Life science is her favorite science. She likes all kinds of animals.

THE SCIENCE MAGNIFIER KIDS IN ... The Observation Deck

BANG!

THE SIREN JUST REMINDS HIM OF A DOG HOWLING. MY BROTHER STUDIES WOLVES, AND HE SAYS HOWLING IS HOW THEY TALK TO EACH OTHER. WOLVES AND DOGS ARE RELATED, YOU KNOW.

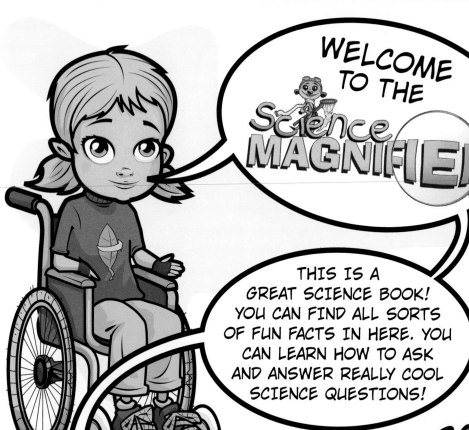

WELCOME TO THE Science MAGNIFIER™

THIS IS A GREAT SCIENCE BOOK! YOU CAN FIND ALL SORTS OF FUN FACTS IN HERE. YOU CAN LEARN HOW TO ASK AND ANSWER REALLY COOL SCIENCE QUESTIONS!

AS YOU READ THE BOOK, YOU WILL SEE SOME FEATURES THAT CAN HELP YOU LOOK AT SCIENCE IN A NEW WAY.

GLAD SCIENTIST

Do your own science investigations. Make predictions, answer questions, and write down your very own results.

MAKE THE CONNECTION

Get out your science notebook and write down your science questions. Explore new ideas using what you have learned.

CHECK YOUR ANSWERS ON PAGES 314–329!

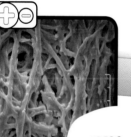

Thinking **BIG**™

www.carolinacurriculum.com/ThinkingBig

THINKING BIG

There is a special kind of microscope that can take pictures of the smallest things.

When you see this feature, look closely at the picture and read the clues to see if you can guess what the object is.

You can also go online to www.carolinacurriculum.com/ThinkingBig to see more pictures. Use the zoom feature to make super-small things really big with just a click!

Quick Question?

QUICK QUESTION

Use the questions to see if you understand what you have read. Check your answers in the Answer Key that begins on page 314.

SAFE SCIENCE

Whenever you see this symbol, read carefully so you can stay safe. Science investigations can be tricky sometimes. Always work safely.

Remember!

Is That a Fact?

IS THAT A FACT?

Sometimes a story that has been told over and over gets its facts all tangled up. This feature will help set the record straight!

Did You Know!

DID YOU KNOW?

This book has so many super-cool tidbits of information, you'll be blown away! Look for this feature to find surprising science facts.

UP FRONT
THE FIRST SECTION OF THE BOOK COVERS THE SCIENCE BASICS. WHAT IS THE SCIENTIFIC METHOD? HOW DO YOU KEEP TRACK OF DATA? LEARN THE BEST WAYS TO STUDY SCIENCE. CHECK IT OUT!

WHAT'S IN THE BACK?
IN THE BACK OF THE BOOK THERE ARE MANY HELPFUL SECTIONS. LEARN HOW SCIENTISTS USE MAPS AND FIND WHAT SCIENCE WORDS MEAN. YOU CAN EVEN MEET SOME COOL SCIENTISTS THAT ARE WORKING RIGHT NOW.

Doing the Work of Scientists

What Questions do Scientists Ask?

Why do insects have six legs? Where does water go when it boils? Is there life on other planets? Scientists wonder about things. They ask questions. Then they try to answer questions. When scientists have new information, they share the information with others.

Some scientists want to know more about living things. They ask questions about plants and animals.

Some scientists ask questions about what things are made of.

Some scientists ask questions about Earth and outer space.

Some scientists ask questions about energy. They study sound, light, and forces.

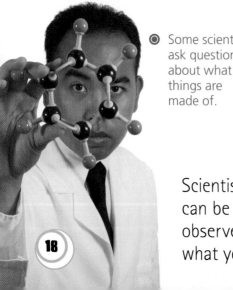

Scientists ask questions about things that can be measured. They ask about things they observe. An **observation** (ob sur VAY shun) is what you see, hear, touch, taste, or smell.

Scientific Method

Scientists use a series of steps to find answers. The steps are called the **scientific method**.

SCIENTIFIC METHOD

THE SCIENCE MAGNIFIER KIDS WILL SHOW YOU HOW THE SCIENTIFIC METHOD WORKS!

1. OBSERVE. THEN ASK A QUESTION

ICE IS SOLID WATER.

I WONDER IF SOLID ICE WEIGHS THE SAME AS LIQUID WATER?

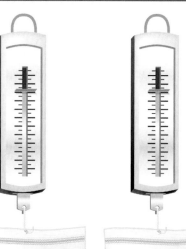

4. DO THE TEST. COLLECT INFORMATION. WRITE YOUR RESULTS IN YOUR SCIENCE NOTEBOOK.

5. TELL PEOPLE ABOUT YOUR RESULTS.

OUR PREDICTION WAS CORRECT.

ICE AND LIQUID WATER WEIGH THE SAME.

6. ASK NEW QUESTIONS.

I WONDER IF LIQUID WATER TAKES UP MORE SPACE THAN ICE?

Keeping a Science Notebook

What Is a Science Notebook?

Scientists collect and **record** (ree KORD) information. When you record information you write it down. This information is called **data**. Keep data in your **science notebook**.

Data are things you can see and measure. An opinion is not data.

measurement

ROCKET WEIGHS 27.5 KILOGRAMS. HE IS 71 CENTIMETERS TALL. HE HAS FOUR LEGS. HE HAS TWO EARS. HIS FUR IS GRAY.

OPINION

ROCKET IS BIG. HIS FUR IS A LIGHT COLOR. SOMETIM HE BARKS. ROCK SLEEPS A LOT.

Set Up Your Notebook

Science notebooks are not all the same. Your teacher may ask you to arrange your science notebook in a certain way. Here is one way to arrange your science notebook:

Write the date. ◉

Write your name.

Rain

Date Sept 18

My Investigation
Is Rocket still getting taller
and heavier?

Write down your science question. This is the beginning of your investigation.

Add a page number.

1

continued

○ Your science notebook will include important records.

Think about your science question. What do you think the answer will be? **Predict** the answer. Write it down.

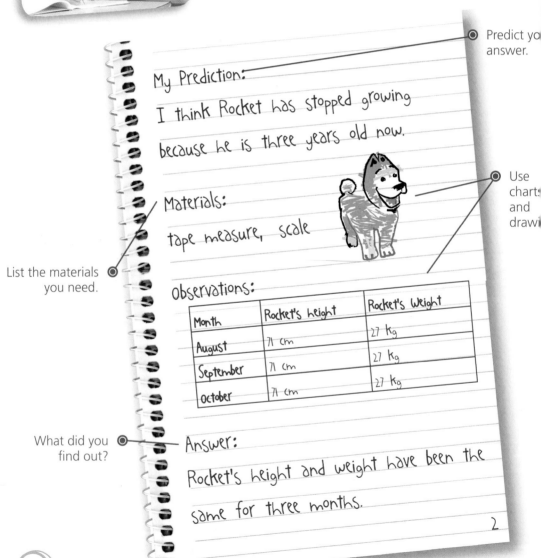

○ Predict your answer.

My Prediction:

I think Rocket has stopped growing because he is three years old now.

Materials:

tape measure, scale

○ List the materials you need.

○ Use charts and draw

Observations:

Month	Rocket's height	Rocket's Weight
August	71 cm	27 kg
September	71 cm	27 kg
October	71 cm	27 kg

○ What did you find out?

Answer:

Rocket's height and weight have been the same for three months.

2

What did you learn? Write your **conclusion**. This is the answer to your question. The data show what the answer should be.

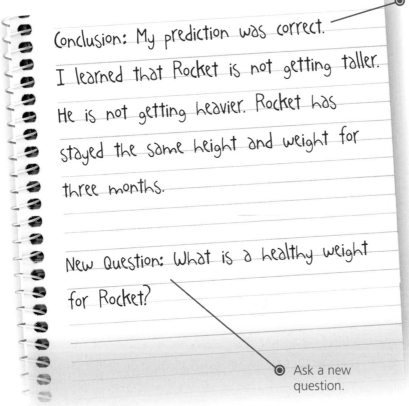

Your conclusion shows what you learned.

Conclusion: My prediction was correct. I learned that Rocket is not getting taller. He is not getting heavier. Rocket has stayed the same height and weight for three months.

New Question: What is a healthy weight for Rocket?

Ask a new question.

You answered one question. Did it make you think of **new questions**?

Organizing Data

What Are Data?

Science information is called **data**. Some data are what you see and notice. These are observations. Other data are measurements. You measure with tools.

OBSERVATION
The zebra is black and white.

MEASUREMENT
The zebra is 140 cm tall.

RAIN GAUGE
Measures how much rain falls.

THERMOMETER
Measures the temperature.

Tables and graphs are a good way to organize data. Tables and graphs can be drawn by hand.

A **tally table** is used to count things. You count things in groups of five. Make a line down for each of the first four things. Then make a line across for the fifth thing. Count up the groups to get a total.

SCIENCE NOTEBOOK

Answers on pages 314–3

HOW MANY ZEBRAS ARE IN THE FIELD?

Animals	Tally
Zebras	‖‖ ‖‖ ‖‖ |||
Giraffes	‖‖	

Tables

A **table** is one way to show data in an organized way.

Think about fast land animals. A table can show their speeds.

The table below is organized by the speed of the animals. The fastest animal is the cheetah. The cheetah is listed first. The slowest animal is the greyhound. It is listed last.

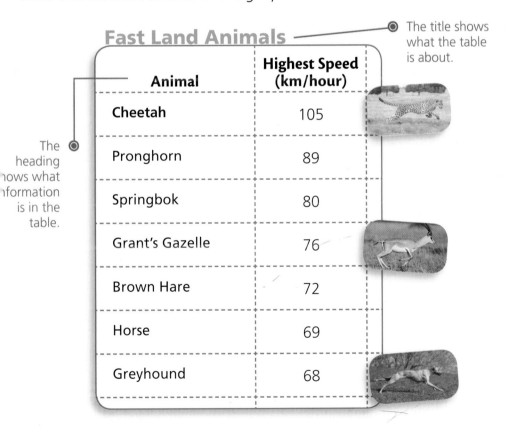

The title shows what the table is about.

The heading shows what information is in the table.

Fast Land Animals

Animal	Highest Speed (km/hour)
Cheetah	105
Pronghorn	89
Springbok	80
Grant's Gazelle	76
Brown Hare	72
Horse	69
Greyhound	68

You can **draw conclusions** from the data. Why do cheetahs eat Grant's gazelles? Because the cheetah can run faster than the gazelles.

Bar Graphs

A **bar graph** helps compare data. The bar graph below shows the same data as the table.

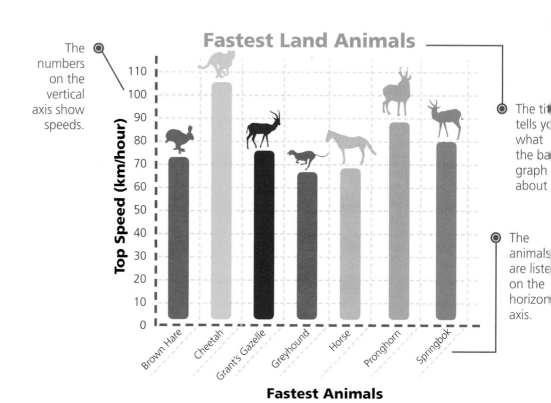

The numbers on the vertical axis show speeds.

Fastest Land Animals

Top Speed (km/hour)

110
100
90
80
70
60
50
40
30
20
10
0

Brown Hare · Cheetah · Grant's Gazelle · Greyhound · Horse · Pronghorn · Springbok

Fastest Animals

The ti[t] tells y[o] what the ba[r] graph [is] about

The animals are liste[d] on the horizon[tal] axis.

The bars on the bar graph show the speed of each animal. Look at the bars and compare the speeds. The bar for the horse is higher than the bar for the greyhound. The horse is faster than the greyhound.

Line Graphs and Pie Graphs

Line graphs show how data change over time. Here is a tally table of butterflies seen in a garden during one week.

Here is the same data in a line graph:

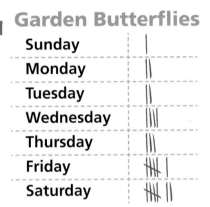

Garden Butterflies

Sunday	|
Monday	||
Tuesday	||
Wednesday	||||
Thursday	|||
Friday	ⅢⅡ |
Saturday	ⅢⅡ ||

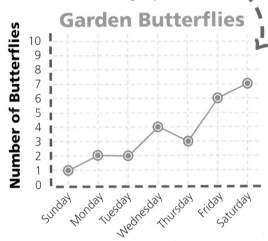

Most butterflies visited the garden late in the week.

Pie graphs compare parts of the total. The parts of a pie graph add up to 100%.

A pie graph looks like a pie that has been cut into pieces.

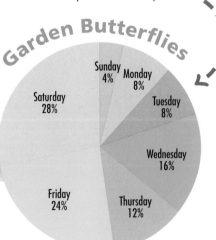

Garden Butterflies

Sunday 4%
Monday 8%
Tuesday 8%
Wednesday 16%
Thursday 12%
Friday 24%
Saturday 28%

Working Safely

What Are Science Safety Rules?

Rules for Safe Science

1. Do not start until your teacher tells you to.

2. Always follow instructions.

3. Get help from an adult if you need it.

4. Wear safety glasses or goggles when needed.

5. Don't put anything in the lab into your mouth. Never taste anything unless your teacher tells you to.

Scienists do not eat or drink anything in the lab!

Lab and Classroom Safety

Rules for a Safe Lab and Classroom

1. Hang up coats, hats, and scarves.

2. Gather the tools you will need before you begin.

3. Be sure to dress for safety. Tie up long hair. Be sure clothing is not loose or hanging in your way.

4. Clean up when you are finished.

⊙ Before you begin your investigation, gather all of your materials.

Tie back loose hair. ⊙

Safe Investigations at Home

Rules for Safe Investigations at Home

1. An adult should work with you.

2. Get everything ready before you start.

3. Dress safely. Tie up long hair. Keep loose clothes out of your way.

4. Keep your work area clean.

5. Clean up spills right away.

6. Recycle plastic, metal, and paper.

Science Safety Outdoors

Rules for Safe Science Outdoors

1. Tell your teacher about any allergies you may have.

2. Stay on the marked path. Do not collect plants or insects.

DON'T TOUCH any OF THESE PLANTS!

poison ivy

poison oak

poison sumac

3. Don't touch a plant you don't know. Some plants have poisonous parts. Watch out for these plants!

4. Stay with your partner. Stay within sight of your teacher or other adults.

◎ This is what a tick looks like.

5. Check your partner for ticks. Look at your shoes, socks, and the legs of your pants.

6. Always be careful around water. Don't fall in! Don't drink outside water. Be careful of animals in water.

Science Tools

What Do Scientists Measure?

Scientists ask a lot of questions. Scientists make observations to answer the questions. They measure things. The measurements must be **accurate**.

◉ You can measure a plant. Use a meterstick, a ruler, or a measuring tape.

Scientists use a lot of tools. They use cameras, prisms, hand lenses and telescopes. They use microscopes to see things that are very small. They use telescopes to see things that are very far away. They use clocks and computers. They use rulers and metersticks. They use thermometers. They use balances and scales.

◉ The scientist can use a thermometer that floats.

You can use a telescope ◉ to see stars, planets, and other things in space.

Making Accurate Measurements

Look at the balloon and the bowling ball. Which one is bigger?

"Which one is bigger?" is not a scientific question. What do you mean by *bigger?*

The balloon takes up more space than the bowling ball. It has more **volume**. Is the balloon bigger than the bowling ball?

The bowling ball has much more stuff in it than the balloon does. It has more **mass**. Is the bowling ball bigger than the balloon?

When you ask a scientific question you must decide what you will measure. Then you must use the right tools to get accurate measurements.

Tools for Measuring

For almost every investigation, there is a science tool to help you.

What You See Some tools help make things look bigger. A **hand lens** makes it easier to see small things. A **microscope** helps you see things that are too small to see with your eyes alone.

◉ You can see details of things with a hand lens.

Hot and Cold **Temperature** is how hot or cold something is. A **thermometer** is a tool that measures temperature.

The red line shows ◉ the temperature.

Graduated Cylinders

Volume The amount of space something takes up is called **volume**. You measure the volume of liquids with a **graduated cylinder**. Liquid volume is measured in **liters** (L).

Length and Distance Rulers and yardsticks measure length. They measure in inches and feet. Scientists use the **metric system**. In the metric system, length is measured in centimeters and meters. You will use a **metric ruler** or a **meterstick** to measure length. Sometimes you will use a **measuring tape**.

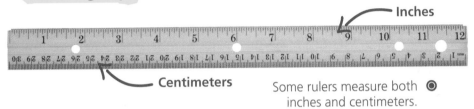

Inches

Centimeters

Some rulers measure both ◉ inches and centimeters.

◉ One side of this measuring tape measures inches and feet. The other side measures centimeters and meters.

Time A **stopwatch** or **clock** can be used to measure time.

◉ This clock can measure seconds, hours, and minutes.

Mass and Weight

Scientists use a **spring scale** to measure weight. You can use a **two-pan balance** or a **triple-beam balance** to measure mass. **Mass** is the amount of matter in an object. Mass is measured in **grams** (g).

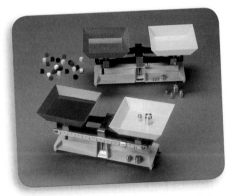

◉ Use a two-pan balance to weigh objects. Put the object on one side and the mass weights on the other.

Technology

What Is Technology?

Technology (tek NAHL uh jee) is another word for tools. We use tools to help solve problems. People have used tools for thousands of years.

○ The first bikes did not have pedals. They did not have brakes. People used technology to improve bicycles.

The first computer weighed ○ 60,000 pounds! The computer you use at school probably weighs about 26 pounds.

Scientists tell other scientists about their discoveries. Sharing ideas helps us learn. Because of technology we can share information instantly. We can use computers. We can use telephones and cell phones.

Technology and Life Science

Technology helps scientists. Sometimes, living things are used to help people. This is called **biotechnology** (by oh tek NAHL uh jee). Scientists use biotechnology to make medicines.

Biotechnology helps make ◉ vaccines and allergy shots

Farmers use technology. Plants use less water. They need less fertilizer. We can grow more food on the same amount of land.

The lettuce is being watered by ◉ drip irrigation. Water is going right to the roots of the lettuce.

The water you drink every day is cleaned by technology. Water treatment plants take out dirt, pesticides, food scraps, soap, and human waste. The water is treated with chlorine. Bacteria eat some of the solid pieces. Clean water is put back into rivers or into the ocean.

◉ Water is tested to make sure it is clean enough to drink.

Technology and Earth Science

Scientists who study Earth are called **geologists** (jee AHL uh jists). Geologists use technology to study how pieces of Earth move around. The movement of Earth causes volcanoes. Earth's movement also causes earthquakes. Scientists are working on technology that will help them predict when earthquakes will happen. Predicting earthquakes will save lives.

Scientists called **meteorologists** (mee tee oh RAHL uh jists) use technology to study weather. They use the information to make the weather reports you watch on television.

This earthquake ◉ monitor gets power from solar energy.

◉ Satellites in space take pictures of weather on Earth.

Technology and Physical Science

Scientists use technology to study energy and motion. Could you fly without an airplane? Technology makes flying possible. We are able to do many things because of technology.

◎ Technology makes it easier to travel. In 1620, it took English settlers on the *Mayflower* 66 days to cross the Atlantic Ocean. Now you can travel from London, England, to New York City in seven hours.

Technology helps people ◎ who have been injured. This man is running on a special kind of artificial leg.

◎ In 1610, Galileo saw the rings around Saturn for the first time. A telescope in space sent back this picture of the rings of Saturn.

You use technology every ◎ day. You may take pictures with a digital camera. You can put the photos on a computer. You can e-mail them to friends.

Systems

What Is a System?

Have you ever played a team sport? Every player on a team has a job to do. A team will not win any games if players are missing.

Every player on a soccer team 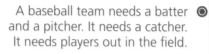 knows how to play the game.

◉ Everyone on a baseball team follows the same rules.

A baseball team needs a batter ◉ and a pitcher. It needs a catcher. It needs players out in the field.

A team is a system. A **system** has parts. All the parts work together. Each part of a system must work for the whole system to work.

The natural world has many systems. Every part of the natural world is part of a system.

Living Systems

A plant is a system. A plant has flowers, leaves, stems, and roots. The plant needs every part to grow and make seeds. A plant needs leaves to use energy from the Sun. A plant needs roots to use water. The body of a cow is a system.

See also:
page
96
Plants

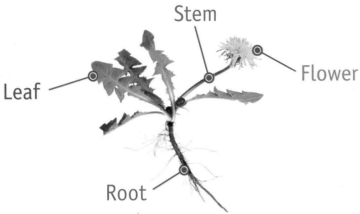

Stem

Flower

Leaf

Root

All the parts of a cow must work for the cow system to work.

See also:
page
56
Organisms

BODY
Food is turned into energy inside the body. The body organs must work for the cow to get energy.

HEAD
The brain of the cow is inside its head. Its ears are here. Its eyes are here. Its mouth is here. The head must work for the cow to think, hear, see, and eat.

LEGS
The cow moves around on its legs. A cow cannot find food without its legs.

Nonliving Systems

The solar system is a natural system. It does not have living parts. The solar system is the Sun, the planets, and everything that moves around the Sun. Earth is part of the solar system.

The solar system is made up of the Sun and all of the planets. Even meteors and moons are part of the solar system.

See also:

page
168
The Solar System

Winds are part of a natural system. Wind does not have living parts.

Strong winds called **trade winds** move ships across the ocean. Air warms up over the ocean. Then heated air rises. Cool air rushes in to take its place. The movement of the air is part of a system that causes winds.

Systems Work Together

Everything is part of a system. The **universe** (YOO nuh vers) is the biggest system that we know of. Everything in space is part of the universe. Earth is part of the universe.

The solar system is a nonliving system. Living systems on Earth need the solar system. If the Sun did not heat Earth, life would not be possible.

Living and nonliving systems work together in an **ecosystem**. Plants need the Sun for energy. Animals—including people—could not live without plants.

See also:
page
122
Ecosystems

Parts of an Ecosystem

SUNLIGHT
All life on Earth needs sunlight.

WATER
All life on Earth needs water.

PLANT
Plants use sunlight and water for energy.

RABBIT
Animals eat plants for energy.

FOX
Some animals eat other animals for energy.

Patterns

What Are Patterns?

A **pattern** is an order of things repeated over and over again. Patterns are all around us.

Some clothes have patterns. This shirt is plaid.

The bricks on this wall form a pattern. Every other line of brick is the same.

There are many patterns in the natural world. Almost everywhere we look in nature, we can find patterns.

The shell of a nautilus grows in a spiral pattern.

No two snowflakes look the same. But every snowflake has the same six-sided pattern.

Bird feathers have a pattern. The feathers on a peacock have a pattern that looks like eyes.

The needles on fir trees grow in a pattern. They grow in rows.

⦿ Sometimes we copy patterns found in nature. The overlapping pattern of snake scales makes the snake waterproof. Sometimes roof shingles are laid in the same pattern.

Thinking **BIG**™

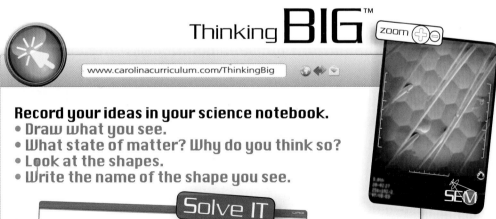

ZOOM ⊕⊖

www.carolinacurriculum.com/ThinkingBig

Record your ideas in your science notebook.
- Draw what you see.
- What state of matter? Why do you think so?
- Look at the shapes.
- Write the name of the shape you see.

Solve IT

1) I am a body part.
2) I am not much use in the dark.
3) I have more lenses than a shoebox full of sunglasses.
4) I belong to a winged insect.

Answers on pages 314–329!

The Pattern of the Sun

The planet Earth spins on its **axis**. The axis is an imaginary line that runs through Earth from the North Pole to the South Pole. It takes 24 hours for Earth to spin all the way around. The spin of Earth is called its **rotation**. Each rotation is called a **day**. The pattern of day and night happens over and over again.

axis

Earth spins like a toy top.

When our side of Earth is pointed toward the Sun, it is day.

When our side of Earth points away from the Sun, it is night.

The Pattern of the Moon

The Moon also spins on an axis. The Moon orbits Earth the way that Earth orbits the Sun. It takes 29.5 days for the Moon to spin all the way around on its axis. It takes the same amount of time for the Moon to spin all the way around Earth. That means that a day and a year are the same on the Moon!

The parts of the Moon that we see are the **phases** of the Moon.

First Quarter

Waxing Gibbous

Waxing Cresent

Full

New

Waning Gibbous

Waning Cresent

Last Quarter

SCIENCE NOTEBOOK

hase of the Moon

ate: December 4

me: 7 p.m.

onditions: clear

oservation: Moon looks

ry full. A sliver of moon

missing. Here's a picture:

⊙ The part of the Moon facing the Sun is lit up. We can see the entire Moon during a **full moon**. The part of the Moon facing away from the Sun is dark. We cannot see the Moon at all during a **new moon**.

Models

What Is a Model?

Scientists like to find out how things work. They make observations. When scientists must observe something that is hard to see, they make a model. A **model** can show what something looks like. A model can show how something works.

Sometimes scientists observe things that are really big, like a planet.

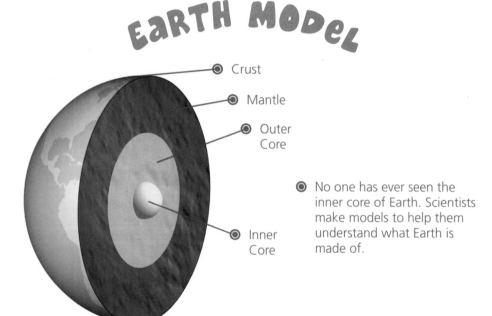

EARTH MODEL

- Crust
- Mantle
- Outer Core
- Inner Core

- No one has ever seen the inner core of Earth. Scientists make models to help them understand what Earth is made of.

Scientists may observe something that has a lot of parts, like an ecosystem.

FOOD WEB MODEL

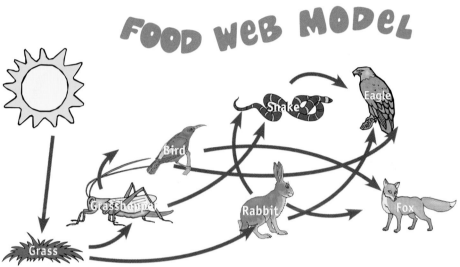

⊙ The model of the food web shows part of an ecosystem. An ecosystem has many parts. The parts depend on each other.

Scientists use models to study small things, too.

GERM MODEL

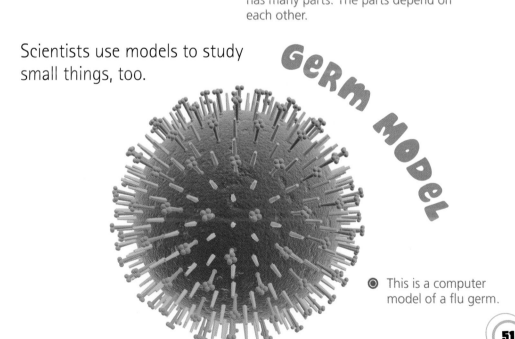

⊙ This is a computer model of a flu germ.

◉ Kinds of Models

Physical Models A model can be a drawing or a diagram.

You can build a model out of wood, paper, clay, or other materials.

◉ This boy built a paper model of an astronaut helmet. The model is the same size as a real helmet.

A dentist uses this model ◉ to show people how to brush teeth. The teeth and the brush are larger than the actual objects.

Mathematical Models
Computers help scientists make mathematical (ma thuh MAT i kul) models.

◉ Computer models are used to help design buildings.

Conceptual Models Sometimes a model is a guess. A scientist asks a question like "what would happen if . . . ?" Then the scientist tries to answer the question.

WHAT WOULD HAPPEN IF . . .

SCHOOL WAS CLOSED FOR A WEEK?

CARS HAD NEVER BEEN INVENTED?

THERE WERE NO HORSES?

Models Have Limits

Models are very useful tools in science. They help us demonstrate how things work. They help us see what things look like.

Sometimes scientific models are not complete. Sometimes models do not work the way they should. Sometimes the model only shows a part of an object or system.

No human has ever seen an actual dinosaur. You have probably seen models of dinosaurs. Scientists have learned about dinosaurs by studying fossils. Fossils cannot tell scientists everything about a dinosaur. For example, fossils cannot show what color dinosaurs were. Scientists make models of what they think the dinosaur looked like.

The first models of the dinosaur called *Brontosaurus* had the wrong head. It was really the head of a dinosaur called *Camarasaurus*. In 1970, scientists discovered that *Brontosaurus* and *Apatosaurus* were the same kind of dinosaur.

Scientists always look for more information. They build better models. They keep learning about the world around them.

Life Science

What is life science? **Life science** is the study of all living things. Living things include plants, bacteria, animals, and people. Would you like to know more about how living things work? Keep reading!

Organisms

What Is an Organism?

What do you have in common with a tree, a fish, and a tiger? All of these things are organisms (OR guh ni zuhmz). You are also an organism. **Organisms** are living things.

All of the living things in this picture are organisms.

You are very different from a tree. You are also very different from a tiger or a fish. But all organisms have some things in common. All living things need energy. They also need air, food, water, and a place to live.

See also:
page
64
Animals

All organisms grow. You are much taller now than when you were a baby. An adult tiger starts as a small tiger cub. All living things can make more living things like themselves. Dogs have puppies. Seeds from sunflowers can become new sunflowers.

What's in a School?

The Place Where You Learn Name the living and nonliving things in your school environment. Write your answers in your science notebook.

FIND ANSWERS ON 314 – 329

Different Kinds of Organisms

Earth has many different kinds of living things. Organisms come in different sizes. Some living things are very small. Other living things, like whales, are huge.

See also:
page
96
Plants

All organisms are made up of tiny building blocks called cells. A **cell** is the smallest part of a living thing.

See also:
page
78
The Human Body

SINGLE CELLED

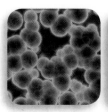 

Bacteria are very small and made of only one cell. You need a microscope to see them.

MANY CELLED

Plants and animals are made up of millions of cells.

Cells have different jobs. But they all work together to keep the organism alive. The cells in your blood, the cells of your stomach, and the cells of your muscles are all different. But when you eat, these cells all help you get the energy you need to ride your bike.

Is That a Fact?

Long Live the Redwoods

Living things have very different lifetimes. The painted lady butterfly lives for about two weeks. But giant redwood trees can live for 2,000 years!

Basic Needs of Organisms

What things do you need to stay alive? You need air to breathe. You need water and food. You need a place to live. All living things need the same things.

○ All living things need energy to live and grow. Animals like this panda get energy from food. Plants get energy from the Sun.

○ These elephants depend on their environment for air, food, water, and a place to live.

See also:
page
88
Food Energy

All living things need a place to live. Some organisms need lots of space to live in. You can keep a pet goldfish in a small bowl. But a whale needs a large part of the ocean.

See also:
page
122
Ecosystems

An **environment** (in VEYE ruh muhnt) is an area made up of living and nonliving things. An organism needs living things such as food. An organism also needs nonliving things such as water and a place to live. You could not live in a lake. A fish could not live in the desert. All organisms have an environment that is just right for them.

Organisms also depend on each other. Animals need other living things for food. Some animals eat plants. Other animals eat animals.

There are other ways that living things need each other. Birds use trees to build nests. Some fish can attach themselves to sharks. The sharks give the fish a place to hide.

This clownfish ◉ depends on the sea anemone for protection and a place to live.

GLaD SCiENTiST

Check your answers, pages 314-329

An Animal Has To Eat!

Can you tell what food these animals eat by looking at their teeth?

1. Look at these two sets of teeth.
2. Make a table with two columns. Label one column "Same" and one column "Different."
3. Under "Same," write down all of the ways these two sets of teeth are the same.
4. Under "Different," write down all of the ways these two sets of teeth are different.
5. Animals that eat plants need teeth that are good for grinding food. Which teeth belong to an animal that eats plants?
6. Animals that eat meat need teeth that can cut and tear. Which teeth belong to an animal that eats meat?
7. Some animals eat both plants and meat. What kind of teeth would this animal have?

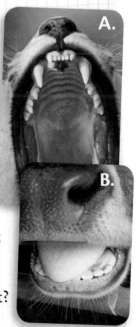

A.

B.

Organisms Grow

When you were born, you were a baby. You could not talk or walk. But you could eat! You kept eating and growing. Soon you could talk and walk. Now you are much bigger than a baby. But you still need to eat, and you are still growing. And even when you are grown, you will continue to change.

All living things grow and change. But they might not grow in the same way. Some young organisms look a lot like adults.

◉ You will keep growing until you are an adult.

A kitten looks ◉ like a small cat.

◉ A calf looks like a small cow.

Other living things change form as they grow. Acorns don't look anything like trees. But an acorn can grow into a large oak tree. A butterfly egg hatches into a caterpillar before it becomes an adult butterfly.

The seeds in this ◉ pumpkin will grow into a new pumpkin.

Organisms Reproduce

All organisms can **reproduce** (ree pruh DOOS). That means they can make more organisms like themselves. These new organisms are called **offspring**. Parent fish have baby fish. Parent flowers have seeds that grow into new flowers.

See also:
page
110
Life Cycles

Do you look like your parents? You probably don't look exactly like either one of them. But you might look similar to your parents because you **inherit** (in HAIR uht) characteristics from both of them. That means that they pass some of their characteristics on to you.

These puppies all ◉ look similar to their mother, but they are not exactly the same.

◉ This baby girl inherited red hair from her mother.

The same is true of all organisms. Zebras all have black and white stripes. But every zebra has a different pattern of stripes. Pea plants all have flowers. But some pea plants have purple flowers and some have white flowers.

◉ Can you see the different pattern of stripes on these zebras?

Organisms Learn to Survive in Their Environment

There are many different places to live on Earth. Some are hot. Some are cold. Some are wet, and some are dry. Each place has its own climate (KLEYE muht). **Climate** is the type of weather a place has.

The organisms that live in different climates have the right body parts and behaviors to live in there.

The red fox has fur that  helps it blend into the forest. Its sight, hearing, and sense of smell help it to catch small animals for its food.

The arctic fox has white fur in the winter that matches the snow and helps it to hide. It likes to store food in secret places to eat during the cold months.

Deserts are hot and dry. Living things in deserts have ways to survive with little water. The kangaroo rat eats dry seeds. The seeds help it make its own water. Some small desert animals stay in shaded spots during the day. The animals come out at night when it is cooler.

A cactus  has special parts to help it store water in the desert.

Some areas are very cold and covered with snow for most of the year. Animals that live in very cold places usually have thick fur to keep them warm.

○ These plants are growing close together and near the ground to protect them from the cold weather.

You cannot live in water, but fish can. Fish have gills that help them breathe in the water. Humans use lungs to breathe on land.

Ducks have webbed feet for swimming. Eagles have claws on their feet to catch food. ○

Thinking BIG™

zoom ⊕⊖

www.carolinacurriculum.com/ThinkingBig

Record your ideas in your science notebook.
• Draw what you see.
• Write two words that tell about the organism.
• How might this animal move? Why?

Solve IT

1) I am a scavenger.
2) I have gills, but I'm not a swimmer.
3) My body is built for rolling.
4) Scientists call me an isopod.

Answers on pages 314–329!

SEM

Animals

What Is an Animal?

What do all of these organisms have in common? They all move differently. They have different body coverings. They live in different places. They eat different kinds of food. They are different sizes. But in one way they are all the same. They are all **animals**.

Monarch butterfly

◉ These organisms are very different, but they are all animals.

Lion

Tarantula

Prairie dog

There are many kinds of animals. But all animals have some things in common. Animals are made of many cells. Animals cannot make their own food. They must eat plants or other animals. Animals can move from place to place. Animals can make new animals.

There are two major groups of animals. One group is made of animals that have backbones. The other group is made of animals that do not have backbones.

Great blue heron

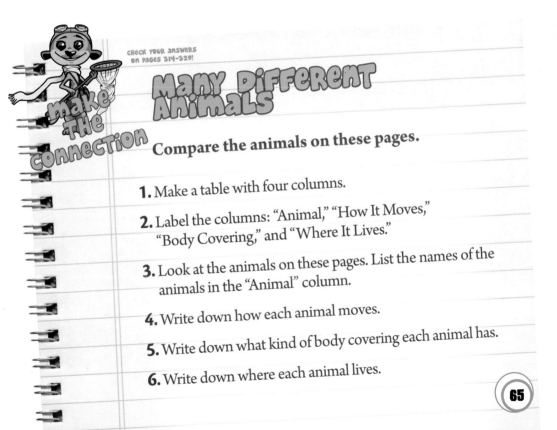

CHECK YOUR ANSWERS on PAGES 314–329!

Many Different Animals

Compare the animals on these pages.

1. Make a table with four columns.

2. Label the columns: "Animal," "How It Moves," "Body Covering," and "Where It Lives."

3. Look at the animals on these pages. List the names of the animals in the "Animal" column.

4. Write down how each animal moves.

5. Write down what kind of body covering each animal has.

6. Write down where each animal lives.

Vertebrates

Animals that have a backbone are called **vertebrates** (VUHR tuh bruhtz). Vertebrates have bones inside their bodies. These bones protect and support them.

There are five types of vertebrates: fish, amphibians, reptiles, birds, and mammals.

See also:
page
56
Organisms

Fish All fish have gills. Gills help fish breathe under the water. Fish have fins and tails that help them swim. Most fish are covered with scales. Some fish lay eggs without shells. Others give birth to live young.

This fish has a backbone.

Amphibians Most young amphibians have gills and live in water. Adult amphibians have lungs and breathe air. Amphibians have thin skin that needs to stay wet. Amphibians lay their eggs in water. Frogs and salamanders are amphibians.

Frogs are amphibians.

Reptiles Reptiles have lungs and thick leathery skin. Some reptiles crawl on their bellies. Some have short legs. Reptiles lay eggs with shells. Snakes, lizards, and alligators are reptiles.

Iguanas are reptiles.

Birds Birds are animals that have feathers that cover their body. They also have wings, two legs, and a beak. Most birds can fly. Some birds, such as penguins, cannot fly. Instead, penguins use their wings to swim. Ducks can fly. But they also use their webbed feet to swim. Birds eat insects, seeds, and berries. All birds lay eggs with hard shells. Chickens, herons, eagles, robins, and turkeys are all birds.

This young robin just hatched from its egg. It will stay in the nest until it can fly.

Mammals Mammals are animals that usually give birth to live young. Mammals have hair or fur on their bodies for at least part of their life. You are a mammal. Dogs, cats, dolphins, bats, and monkeys are all mammals.

All young mammals get milk from their mother.

See also:
page
78
The Human Body

History Makers

Jane Goodall (1934–present)

Jane Goodall loves animals. When she was a child, she dreamed of going to Africa. Jane's dream came true! She went to Africa and watched chimpanzees. She still studies them today. Jane Goodall has learned a lot about chimpanzees. She learned that they make tools and hunt for meat. She also learned that each chimpanzee has its own personality.

Invertebrates

Animals that do not have backbones are called **invertebrates** (in VUHR tuh britz). Invertebrates do not have bones inside their bodies.

Most of the animals on Earth are invertebrates. Insects, spiders, worms, jellyfish, and lobsters are invertebrates. None of these animals has a backbone.

◉ An earthworm is an invertebrate. It has no backbone.

Many invertebrates have a hard outside cover. Snails have shells to protect their soft bodies. Beetles and crabs have a hard cover, like a suit of armor.

Snails and crabs ◉ have a hard outer cover for protection.

Thinking **BIG**™

zoom ⊕ ⊖

www.carolinacurriculum.com/ThinkingBig

Record your ideas in your science notebook.
- **What is the first pattern you see?**
- **Might this be manmade, or found in nature?**
- **Why do you think so?**
- **How do you think it feels? Why?**

Solve IT

1) In this sample I am protection.
2) Find me in an aquatic habitat.
3) What am I?

Answers on pages 314–329!

Some invertebrates have no hard covering at all. Worms, octopuses, and jellyfish do not have a hard cover. Many of these animals live in water or live underground. This keeps them from drying out in the Sun.

See also: page **56**

Organisms

◉ Jellyfish live in water.

Insects are the largest group of invertebrates. Insects have six legs and one or two pairs of wings. Flies, ants, butterflies, and bees are insects.

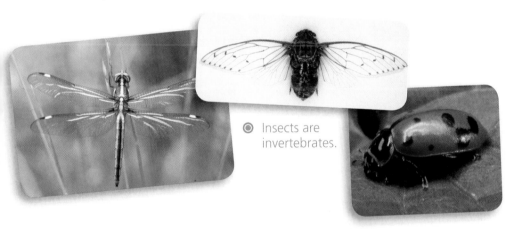

◉ Insects are invertebrates.

GO ONLINE

To learn more about wildlife, check out this Web site!

• **National Wildlife Federation**
http://www.nwf.org/wildlife/

Habitat

See also:
page
122
Ecosystems

Animals can be found all over Earth. Each animal has its own habitat. A **habitat** is a place where an animal lives and gets all of the things it needs. Habitats give animals food, water, space, and a place to live.

WHAT THINGS ARE IN A HABITAT?

Living Things and Nonliving Things

Mountains

Lake

Owls in a tree

Cave

Wildflowers

Bee on a flower

◉ Bats live in caves.

Animals need other living things. Animals get their food from plants and other animals.

Nonliving things can give an animal shelter. Worms live in the ground. Birds build nests out of sticks and mud.

What Do Animals Need?

Name the things that animals need in their habitat. Write your answers in your science notebook.

Find answers on
314 - 329

See also:
page
186

Weather, Seasons, and Climate

A polar bear lives in a cold habitat. Polar bears have thick, white fur that helps them stay warm. The fur's white color also helps the polar bear hide in the snow. Polar bears often eat fish from the cold waters in their habitat. Polar bears could not live in a hot habitat.

A hummingbird and a parrot are both birds. They both have wings and fly. But they have very different beaks. This is because they eat different types of food. A hummingbird needs a habitat with lots of flowers. A parrot needs a habitat with lots of seeds and nuts.

◉ Hummingbirds have long beaks to reach food in flowers.

◉ Parrots have beaks to break open seeds and nuts.

GLAD SCIENTIST

CHECK YOUR ANSWERS, PAGES 314-329!

BACKYARD SAFARI

Explore habitats in your neighborhood.

1. Think about your neighborhood. Describe the type of habitat you live in. Ask yourself these questions:
   a. What kind of weather do you have? Does it stay the same all year?
   b. What are the living and nonliving things around you? Do you live in the mountains or near the ocean? Do you live in the city or near a forest?
2. What wild animals live in this habitat?
3. What things help these animals live in their habitat?
4. What can we learn about humans when we study animals?

71

Animal Behavior

Animals have body parts that help them survive in their habitat. To survive means to stay alive. Animals also do things to help them survive. This is called **behavior** (bee HAY vyer).

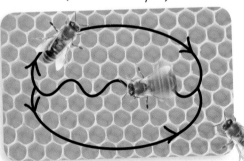

Some behaviors help animals find food. For instance, honeybees do a dance to tell other bees in the hive where to find flowers.

◉ A bee's dance pattern helps the other bees find food.

◉ This chimpanzee is using a stick to get food from an anthill.

Is That a Fact?

People Places

Humans are animals that can live in many different habitats. That's because we can change our behavior. When it's cold, we can dress in warm clothes and heat our homes. When it's hot, we can find ways to stay cool. We have learned to grow food in areas with little water. Humans have made tools and machines to help us survive in many places on Earth and even in space!

Some behaviors help animals survive when the weather changes. In the winter, some birds fly south to warmer areas. This is called **migration** (meye GRAY shuhn). They fly back north in the spring when the weather is warm again.

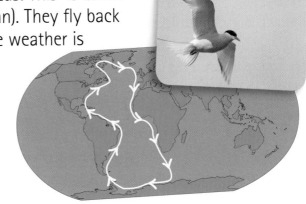

Geese fly in a V pattern ◉ when they migrate south in winter.

◉ The arctic tern migrates farther than any other animal. It flies over 16 kilometers (10,000 miles) from the Arctic to Antarctica. Then it flies back in the spring!

The animals that do not migrate might not find much food in the winter. These animals eat a lot in the summer and fall. Then they **hibernate** in the winter in a hole or den. This means they go into a deep rest or sleep. Gophers and frogs hibernate.

GO ONLINE

To learn more about chimpanzees, check out this Web site!

- **Discover Chimpanzees**
  http://www.discoverchimpanzees.org

Endangered Species and Extinction

A habitat can sometimes change. Then an animal cannot live there. Sometimes there is a forest fire. Then the animals that live in the forest will not be able to find food. They will not be able to find a place to live. Some animals will die. Others will move.

Sometimes a habitat has too many changes. Animals can then become extinct (ik STINKT). **Extinct** animals are animals that do not exist, or live, anywhere.

◉ Both of these animals once lived on Earth. They are now extinct.

Diplodocus

Wooly mammoth

Other animals are extinct too. Passenger pigeons once lived in our forests. People began to cut down trees to build houses. The birds had to find other places to live and get food. Then hunters started shooting the birds for food. The last passenger pigeon on Earth died in a zoo.

People now protect animals that might become extinct. These animals are called **endangered** (in DAYN juhrd) **species** (SPEE sheez). The Asian elephant, Atlantic salmon, and gray wolf are all endangered animals.

◉ The gray wolf is endangered.

Some animals are no longer endangered. People have protected them. The bald eagle and American alligator are not on the list of endangered species anymore.

See also:
page
56
Organisms

GO ONLINE

To learn more about passenger pigeons, check out this Web site!

• **The Passenger Pigeon**
http://www.si.edu/Encyclopedia_SI/nmnh/passpig.htm

77

The Human Body

What Is the Human Body?

What have you done today? You woke up. You brushed your teeth. You had breakfast. You came to school. Now you are reading. You can do all of these things because of your amazing human body!

Your body moves. You control many of the movements. You can raise your hand. You can smile. You can jump and run. You can sing and shout. You can do all of these things when you want to.

The human body can do some amazing things!

Your body does some things on its own. Your heart pumps blood without stopping. Your lungs breathe in and out. Your brain sends signals to all the parts of your body. You don't have to think about doing these things.

Your body gets energy from the food you eat. The body uses this energy for everything it does. The body also uses food to build and repair the body. That is why it is important to eat healthy foods.

See also:
page
88

Food Energy

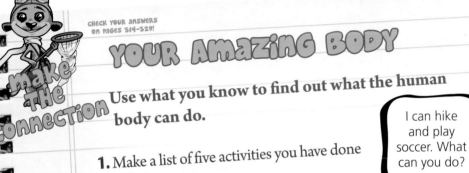

CHECK YOUR ANSWERS ON PAGES 314-329!

YOUR AMAZING BODY

make the connection

Use what you know to find out what the human body can do.

1. Make a list of five activities you have done today.

2. What body parts did you use in each activity? Write the names of these body parts next to each activity.

3. What is the most amazing thing your body can do? Why do you think it is the most amazing thing?

I can hike and play soccer. What can you do?

Organs and Organ Systems

Your body contains many different organs. An **organ** is a part of the body that does a special job.

Your heart is an organ. Its job is to pump blood through the body. Your lungs are also organs. They have the job of breathing in and out.

Organs work together in groups called **organ systems**. All of the organ systems in your body work together.

MRI scan

Heart

Lungs

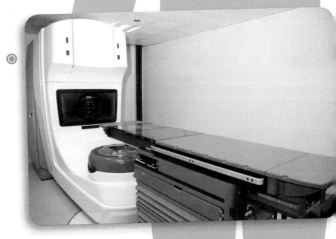

Doctors and scientists can look at organs with special tools like this MRI machine.

Organ System	What the Organ System Does	Parts of the Organ System
Respiratory System	Helps you breathe	Lungs Nose
Circulatory System	Helps blood get to all parts of your body	Heart Blood vessels
Nervous System	Helps control your actions	Brain Spinal cord Nerves
Skeletal System	Helps hold you up and protects parts inside your body	Bones Skull Spine
Muscular System	Helps you move	Muscles
Digestive System	Helps you get energy	Mouth Stomach Intestines

Kari breathes through her nose.

Kari's bones are holding her up.

Kari's stomach helps her digest food.

See also:
page
56
Organisms

Which-Is-Which?

BRAIN STOMACH NOSE

HEART MUSCLES

Name the organ system that goes with each body part listed above. Write your answers in your science notebook.

FIND ANSWERS ON 314 – 329

Skeletal System

See also:
page
56
Organisms

Imagine what would happen if you did not have bones. You would be a big pile of mush! It's a good thing you have a skeletal (SKE luh tuhl) system. Your **skeletal system** includes the skull, the backbone, and all of the bones in your body. Your **bones** support and give shape to your body. They also work with muscles so that you can move.

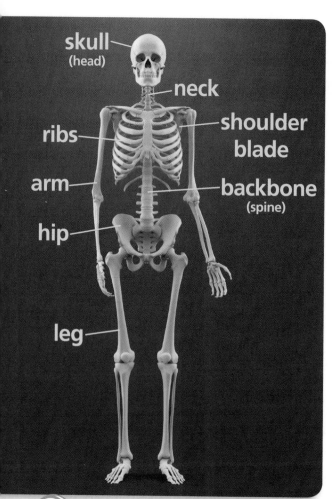

skull
(head)

neck

ribs

shoulder
blade

arm

backbone
(spine)

hip

leg

The skeletal system also protects the inside of your body. Your skull covers your **brain**. Your backbone covers your **spinal cord**. Your ribs protect your **heart** and **lungs**.

The bones of your body are very hard and strong. That is why they can support and protect your body. To keep bones strong, it is important to eat healthy foods. Milk, yogurt, and other dairy foods help keep your bones healthy.

Bones don't bend, but you can bend your body at certain places. These places are called joints. A **joint** is where two bones come together. Your elbows, knees, shoulders, and ankles are some of the joints in your body.

Different joints move in different ways. The names of the joints describe the way that each type of joint moves.

Type of Joint	How It Moves	Examples
Gliding Joint	The bones of this joint glide over one another.	Wrist Ankle
Hinge Joint	This joint moves like the hinge of a door.	Elbow Knee
Ball-and-Socket Joint	This joint allows the bones to move in a full circle.	Shoulder Hip

Socket

Ball

◉ This X-ray shows the ball-and-socket joint of a shoulder. The top of the arm is the "ball." It fits into the shoulder, which is the "socket."

An elbow ◉ bends like the hinge of a door.

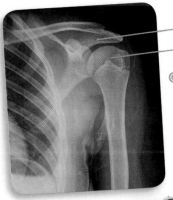

◉ The ball-and-socket joint of a tripod lets you move your camera in every direction.

Muscular System

Bones support your body, but they can't move on their own. You can move your bones because they are attached to muscles. **Muscles** belong to the organ system called the **muscular** (MUHS kyoo ler) **system**.

How do muscles work? Think of a rubber band. When you pull on a rubber band, it stretches and gets longer. If you let it go, it gets shorter. Muscles move by stretching and shrinking, like rubber bands. Muscles are attached to bones. When muscles stretch and shrink, they pull bones to make them move.

Your body has three types of muscles.

Type of Muscle	What Is It?	Examples
Skeletal Muscle	Is attached to the bones to help them move	
Smooth Muscle	Is found in the walls of some organs, such as the stomach	
Heart Muscle	Makes your heart beat automatically	

Skeletal muscles in  your legs let you run.

◎ Your heart is made of heart muscle. It pumps blood through your body so all of your other muscles can work.

Did You Know?

There are more than 30 muscles in just your face! These muscles let you be silly.

GLaD SCiENTiST

CHECK YOUR ANSWERS, PAGES 314–329!

MiGHTY MUSCLe!

Find out how your muscles work.

1. Hold your arm straight down on your side. Feel the biceps muscle, which is at the top and front of your arm. How does it feel?
2. Now pick up a book, bend your elbow, and raise the book. How does your biceps muscle feel now? Did the muscle get shorter or longer?
3. What can you do to make other muscles in your body shorten and lengthen?

Digestive System

Your body gets energy from the food you eat. But first the food must be broken down into parts. The organ system that breaks food down is called the **digestive** (dy JES tiv) **system**.

Many different organs work together to break down food. The digestive system keeps what your body needs. It gets rid of the things your body doesn't need.

◉ Take time to chew your food well.

Chewing your food breaks it into smaller pieces. These pieces are mixed with **saliva**, a digestive juice in your mouth.

How does the digestive system break down food?

1 Food enters your body through your mouth. Your teeth break the food into smaller pieces. Your tongue helps you swallow.

2 After you swallow, the food goes down a long tube called the **esophagus**.

3 Muscles in the **stomach** help mix the food.

4 The food enters the **small intestine** and then the **large intestine**. The body keeps the nutrients it needs and gets rid of the things it doesn't need.

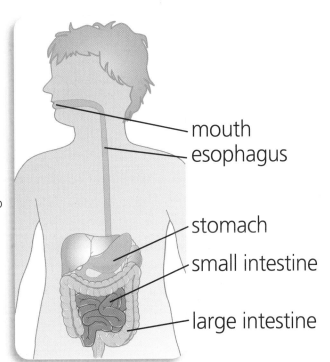

mouth
esophagus

stomach

small intestine

large intestine

Is That a Fact?

Small but Super Long

The small intestine is called "small" because it is not as wide as the large intestine. But it is really pretty big. If you stretched your small intestine out, it would be 7 meters (21 feet) long!

GO ONLINE

To learn more about your body, check out these Web sites!

- **How the Body Works**
  http://kidshealth.org/kid/htbw/

- **Wilhelm Röentgen**
  http://nobelprize.org/nobel_prizes/physics/laureates/1901/rontgen-bio.html

Food Energy

What Is Food Energy?

Imagine that you are going to explore a dark cave. Your friend hands you a flashlight. But when you turn on the switch, there is no light! What is wrong? You open the flashlight, and there are no batteries inside!

A flashlight needs energy from its batteries to make light. You need energy to do all of the things your body does, too. But you don't get your energy from batteries. You get your energy from food.

Just like a ◉ flashlight gets energy from batteries, you get your energy from food.

There is energy in food. This energy is measured in a special unit called **calories** (KAL uh reez). Each type of food has different amounts of calories.

Your body uses the calories from food to do the things that it needs to do. Your body needs energy to breathe. It needs energy to keep your heart beating. Your body needs energy to grow and repair itself. It needs energy to move, sleep, and eat. Food helps your body do all of these different things.

See also:
page
220
Energy

◎ You get calories from the foods you eat. You use this energy for everything you do.

GO ONLINE

To learn more about food energy, check out these Web sites!

- **My Pyramid for Kids**
  http://www.mypyramid.gov/Kids/kids_game.html
- **Figuring Out Food Labels**
  http://kidshealth.org/kid/stay_healthy/food/labels.html

Nutrients

See also:
page
78
The
Human
Body

There are six important nutrients (NOO tree uhnts). **Nutrients** are the parts of food that help you to grow and stay healthy. Your body needs many different types of nutrients to work properly. Most foods have more than one type of nutrient.

Carbohydrates Carbohydrates (kar boh HY drayts) give you energy. You get carbohydrates from eating bread, rice, pasta, and potatoes. Vegetables and fruits also have carbohydrates.

Fruits, vegetables, and grains have carbohydrates.

Fats can be liquid, like olive oil, or solid, like butter.

Fats Fats also give you energy. Milk, cheese, and meat all contain fat. Nuts, peanut butter, and olive oil also contain fat. Your body needs a little bit of fat to stay healthy. But eating too much fat is not good for you.

What Are the Nutrients?

Healthy Body Name the six nutrients we need to stay healthy. Write your answer in your science notebook.

find answers on
514 - 529

Proteins Milk, beans, meat, fish, and eggs are some of the foods that have proteins. Protein helps build strong muscles.

◎ Protein is a nutrient that is found in many types of foods.

Water We need water more than we need any other nutrient. Your body needs water to work. You get water from the foods you eat and the things you drink. But the best way to get enough water is to drink water!

Vitamins Vitamins help keep us healthy. There are vitamins in most of the foods we eat.

It is important to ◎ drink plenty of water, especially after exercise.

The calcium ◎ in milk helps build strong bones and teeth.

Minerals Minerals also help keep us healthy. Many foods have calcium and iron.

Some Important Vitamins

VITAMIN A

Spinach help keep eyes healthy.

VITAMIN C

Strawberries help fight colds.

VITAMIN D

Salmon helps grow strong bones.

◎ Food Pyramid

The **Food Pyramid** shows which foods you should eat every day to be healthy.

MyPyramid

MyPyramid.gov

GRAINS | VEGETABLES | FRUITS | MILK | MEAT & BEANS

The pyramid has six stripes with different colors. Each color stands for one of the six food groups. You should eat food from each stripe every day. Some stripes are wider than others are. You should eat more foods from the wider stripes.

The person climbing the pyramid helps remind you that exercise also keeps you healthy.

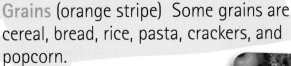

Grain group

Vegetable group

Grains (orange stripe) Some grains are cereal, bread, rice, pasta, crackers, and popcorn.

Vegetables (green stripe) It is good to eat different colored vegetables. Some vegetables are carrots, broccoli, peas, sweet potatoes, and lettuce.

Fruits (red stripe) Some fruits are apples, bananas, cherries, grapes, and oranges. Fruit juice is also included in this group.

it group

Milk group

Milk (blue stripe) This group includes dairy foods like milk, yogurt, and cheese.

Meat and Beans (purple stripe) This group has foods with lots of protein. Some foods in this group are chicken, fish, meat, nuts, and eggs.

Meats and beans group

Fats and Oils (yellow stripe) This is not really a food group, but you do need a little fat each day. The best fats are liquid oils, such as olive oil or corn oil.

Healthy Eating

All packaged foods have a **Nutrition Facts** label. This label describes the nutrients and calories in the food.

See also:
page
78
The Human Body

How much food is in one serving

How many calories are in one serving

How many nutrients are in one serving

How many servings are in the package

How many calories come from fat

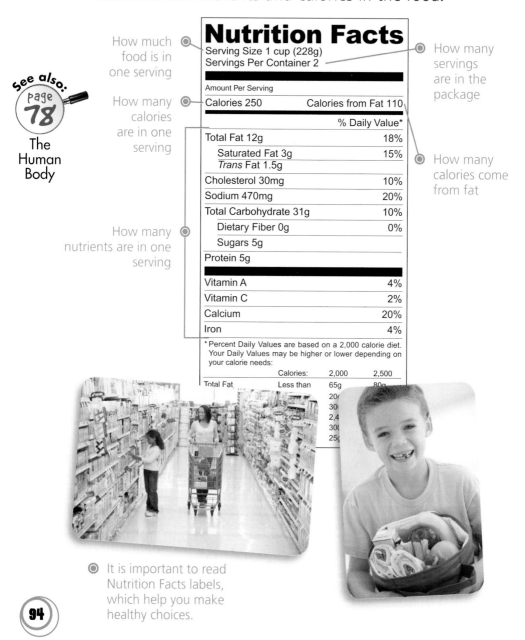

Nutrition Facts

Serving Size 1 cup (228g)
Servings Per Container 2

Amount Per Serving	
Calories 250	Calories from Fat 110

	% Daily Value*
Total Fat 12g	18%
Saturated Fat 3g	15%
Trans Fat 1.5g	
Cholesterol 30mg	10%
Sodium 470mg	20%
Total Carbohydrate 31g	10%
Dietary Fiber 0g	0%
Sugars 5g	
Protein 5g	
Vitamin A	4%
Vitamin C	2%
Calcium	20%
Iron	4%

* Percent Daily Values are based on a 2,000 calorie diet. Your Daily Values may be higher or lower depending on your calorie needs:

	Calories:	2,000	2,500
Total Fat	Less than	65g	80g
		20	30
		30	2,4
		300	25g

It is important to read Nutrition Facts labels, which help you make healthy choices.

Some foods are better for your body than other foods. Be sure to read food labels. Look for *whole grain* or *low fat* on the label. Look at the ingredients list. Try not to choose foods with sugar or corn syrup near the top of the list.

MAKE HEALTHY CHOICES

- Eat breakfast every day.
- Try to eat whole grain cereals and breads.
- Eat lots of vegetables and fruit.
- Have at least two cups of low-fat or fat-free milk a day.
- Drink plenty of water.
- Choose foods and drinks that are low in sugar.
- Choose foods that are low in fat.

CHECK YOUR ANSWERS ON PAGES 314–329!

SNACK ATTACK!

make THE connection

Use what you know about healthy eating to choose a snack.

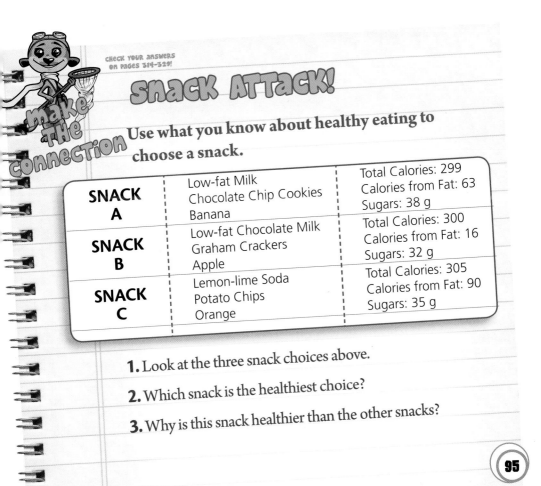

SNACK A	Low-fat Milk Chocolate Chip Cookies Banana	Total Calories: 299 Calories from Fat: 63 Sugars: 38 g
SNACK B	Low-fat Chocolate Milk Graham Crackers Apple	Total Calories: 300 Calories from Fat: 16 Sugars: 32 g
SNACK C	Lemon-lime Soda Potato Chips Orange	Total Calories: 305 Calories from Fat: 90 Sugars: 35 g

1. Look at the three snack choices above.

2. Which snack is the healthiest choice?

3. Why is this snack healthier than the other snacks?

Plants

What Is a Plant?

There are many different kinds of plants. They come in different shapes and sizes. Some plants are tall—like trees. Other plants are very small—like mosses. Some plants have large leaves. Other plants have thin, spiky leaves. Some plants live in very dry areas. Other plants live in water. But what is a plant?

◉ Different kinds of plants have different kinds of leaves.

See also:
page
56
Organisms

A plant is an organism that is made of many cells. Like all living things, plants need energy and a place to live. Plants also need water, air, and nutrients from their environment. And all plants grow and can make new plants. But unlike other living things, **plants** make their own food. Plants use sunlight, water, and air to make food.

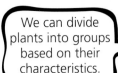

We can divide plants into groups based on their characteristics.

Flowering Plants

Many plants have flowers.

Nonflowering Plants

Some plants do not have flowers.

Deciduous

Some plants have leaves that turn colors and fall off each autumn.

Evergreens

Some plants keep their leaves all year, even in winter.

GO ONLINE

Thinking **BIG**™

Look online for a micrograph of a Bee Leg with Pollen, a Flower Bud, a Flower Petal, and Plant Roots:
http://www.carolinacurriculum.com/ThinkingBig.

Photosynthesis

Plant cells are different from other cells. Plant cells have a cell wall. Cell walls help protect and support the plant. Plant cells also have chlorophyll (KLOR uh fil). **Chlorophyll** is what gives plants their green color.

See also:
page
238
Light

Chlorophyll absorbs light energy from the Sun. Plants use this energy to make their own food. They do this through a process called **photosynthesis** (foh toh SIN thuh sis). This is what makes plants different from other living things.

PHOTOSYNTHESIS

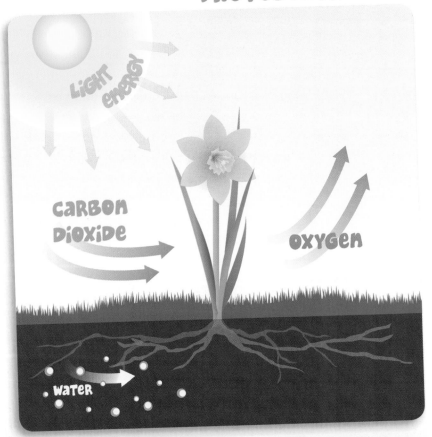

LIGHT energy

carbon dioxide

oxygen

water

In photosynthesis, plants use the energy of the Sun to combine water and carbon dioxide and make it into food. The food made by plants is a kind of sugar called **glucose** (GLOO cos). When plants make glucose, they also make oxygen that is released into the air.

GLAD SCIENTIST

CHECK YOUR ANSWERS
PAGES 314-329

LET THE SUN SHINE

Discover the importance of light on plants.

1. Plant two plants of the same kind in two separate pots.
2. Water the plants with the same amount of water.
3. Place both plants in a sunny spot. Put a cardboard box over one of the plants.
4. Water the plants with the same amount of water every day. After watering, replace the box over the plant that is covered.
5. Each day for two weeks, look at the plants. Write down what the plants look like each day.
6. At the end of two weeks, which plant looks healthier? Why?
7. The only difference between the two plants is the amount of sunlight they received. What happens to a plant that does not get sunlight?
8. Why is sunlight important for plants?

Plant Structures

Plants have special parts that help them live and grow. These are leaves, roots, and stems. Some plants also have flowers.

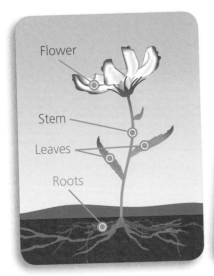

Flower

Stem

Leaves

Roots

Leaves Leaves capture energy from the Sun. Leaves also take in carbon dioxide from the air.

◎ The leaf is where plants make their food through photosynthesis.

Stems Stems support the plant. Stems hold the leaves up so that they can get sunlight. Stems also carry water and nutrients through the plant from the roots to the leaves.

Roots Roots hold plants in the ground. Roots also take in water and nutrients from the soil.

Flowers Some plants have flowers. Flowers can make plants very pretty. But flowers also help plants reproduce. In other words, flowers help plants make more plants.

Roots carry ◎ water and nutrients to the other parts of the plant through the stem.

Plant Growth

Seeds don't look like they could be alive. But put a seed in some soil, and give it the water and temperature it needs. You will soon have a plant that looks very alive. You may even have some great vegetables to eat or flowers to look at!

See also:
page
110

Life Cycles

If a seed has the right environment, it will germinate (JER muh nayt). To **germinate** means a plant will start to grow. First the hard covering of a seed splits open. Then the first small root grows into the soil. The root keeps growing, and the plant pushes out of the soil. Small leaves begin to grow and get larger as the plant gets bigger.

Inside every seed is a tiny plant that can grow if you plant it and care for it.

First, the plant sprouts. Then it becomes a seedling. The plant will continue to grow. Soon the plant will be able to reproduce and make seeds. When these new seeds fall to the ground, more plants can grow.

ALL KINDS OF PLANTS MAKE ALL KINDS OF GARDENS. WHAT IS IN A FLOWER GARDEN? YOU MIGHT FIND PLANTS THAT HAVE NECTAR, A SUGARY FOOD FOR BEES AND BUTTERFLIES. HERB GARDENS HAVE PLANTS, SUCH AS BASIL, THAT WE USE TO MAKE OUR FOOD TASTE GOOD. AND IT'S FUN TO EAT FOODS, SUCH AS TOMATOES AND PEPPERS, THAT WE GROW IN OUR OWN VEGETABLE GARDENS AT HOME.

make the connection

CHECK YOUR ANSWERS ON PAGES 314-329!

WHICH WAY IS UP?

Watch the effects of gravity on a plant.

1. Take a potted plant, and place it on its side.

2. Make sure the plant gets enough water and sunlight.

3. Each day for two weeks, look at the plant. Write down or draw what the plant looks like each day.

4. How has the plant changed?

5. Gravity pulls things down to the ground. Is the plant growing in the same direction as gravity or in the opposite direction?

Plant Reproduction

Many plants make more plants using seeds. Flowering plants make more plants with flowers and fruits. Flowers are where seeds are formed. The flowers have special parts to make seeds.

THE STIGMA IS STICKY. THIS IS WHERE THE POLLEN LANDS.

THE STAMENS MAKE A POWDER CALLED POLLEN.

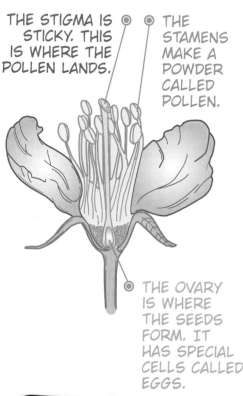

THE OVARY IS WHERE THE SEEDS FORM. IT HAS SPECIAL CELLS CALLED EGGS.

Many plants need animals, like bees, for pollination. **Pollination** (pah luh NAY shuhn) happens when **pollen** gets to the **ovary** of the flower. A bee is attracted to the flower by its colorful petals. Some of the pollen from the **stamens** sticks to the bee. The bee flies from flower to flower carrying pollen. Some of the pollen rubs off onto the **stigma**. Then the pollen moves down the tube into the ovary to join with the eggs. When this happens, seeds are formed.

As the seeds grow, the flower petals fall away. The ovary becomes a fruit. The fruit falls off the plant. Then the seeds land in soil where they grow and make new plants.

◉ When seeds form, the ovaries of orange tree flowers become oranges.

The seeds of other plants are found in **cones**. Evergreen trees make seeds this way. Pinecones hold the seeds to make new pine trees. When the pinecone opens up, the seeds fall out.

Club mosses ◉ have spores instead of seeds.

Some plants, like mosses and ferns, do not have seeds. How do they make new plants? These plants have **spores**. Spores are not made in flowers or cones. But like seeds, spores grow into new plants.

Thinking **BIG**™ zoom ⊕⊖

www.carolinacurriculum.com/ThinkingBig

Record your ideas in your science notebook.
• **What do you see?**
• **Might the object be living or nonliving?**
• **Why do you think so?**

SEM

Solve IT

1) I'm a beginning and end.
2) I have a coat that doesn't zip.
3) I am part of a life cycle.
4) Food is inside me.
5) A baby plant is inside.
6) What am I?

Answers on pages 314–329!

BEES ARE INSECTS. THEY HAVE SIX LEGS AND FOUR WINGS. WHEN BEES FLAP THEIR WINGS QUICKLY, THEY MAKE A BUZZING SOUND.

BEES HAVE TWO ANTENNAE THAT THEY USE TO SMELL. THEY ALSO HAVE A STINGER. SO DON'T BOTHER A BEE—IT MAY STING YOU!

WHEN A BEE FLIES ONTO A FLOWER PETAL, THE POLLEN STICKS TO ITS FUZZY BODY. THEN THE BEE FLIES TO ANOTHER FLOWER, AND SOME OF THE POLLEN FALLS OFF. THIS IS HOW FLOWERS MAKE SEEDS.

Plants and Their Environment

Plants grow in almost every place on Earth. Each type of plant has an environment that is best for it to grow. Plants need the right amount of sunlight, water, and nutrients to make seeds and grow.

⊙ Cactuses have thick stems that store water. This helps them to survive in dry, hot deserts.

⊙ Plants that live in rocky areas have small roots that don't need to reach deep into the ground.

⊙ Some plants need lots of water. These plants grow in wetlands.

Plants depend on other living things. Insects spread pollen from plant to plant. Animals often carry seeds away from plants and drop them in places where they can grow.

Plants are also important parts of their environment. Plants are food for animals. Plants put oxygen into the air. Plants also keep the soil from being washed away by water or wind.

Plants provide ⊙ homes for many animals.

Plants respond to their environment. Light, gravity, and changing seasons are some of the things that affect plants.

Have you ever seen a plant bending toward a sunny window? Plants grow toward light.

How do plant stems know to grow up from the ground? Plants respond to gravity. **Gravity** is the force that pulls things toward the center of Earth.

◎ This tree changes each season. It is responding to changes in the amount of daylight.

The roots of this sunflower ◎ grow down, in the same direction as the pull of gravity. The stem grows up, in the opposite direction of the pull of gravity.

Plants also respond to seasons. In summer, the days are long and the nights are short. In fall, the days get shorter and the nights get longer. The changes in the amount of daylight affect many kinds of plants.

GO ONLINE

To find out more about plants, visit these Web sites!
- **The Great Plant Escape**
  http://urbanext.illinois.edu/gpe/
- **Meat-Eating Plants**
  http://kids.nationalgeographic.com/Stories/AnimalsNature/Meat-eating-plants

Life Cycles

What Is a Life Cycle?

A **life cycle** is all of the changes a living thing goes through from birth to death. All life cycles have a pattern. That pattern consists of birth, becoming an adult, reproduction, and death. Then the pattern starts over again.

See also:
page
56
Organisms

Birth All living things must begin life. Some simple organisms split off from an adult organism. Other living things begin life as seeds. Some living things hatch from eggs. Humans and many other animals grow inside their mothers before they are born alive.

◎ These babies grew inside their mothers before they were born.

What Is the Life Cycle?

The Circle of Life Name the four parts of a life cycle. Write your answer in your science notebook.

FIND ANSWERS ON 314 - 329

◉ All living things are born and grow into adults.

See also: page **46** Patterns

Becoming an Adult All living things grow and change to become adults. Sometimes this happens very quickly. Ladybugs go from egg to adult in about one month. But it takes some organisms a long time to become an adult. Elephants take about 11 years to become adults! Sometimes organisms don't change much as they become adults. Other organisms change a lot.

Gorilla and baby

Young plant

Adult plant

continued (111)

Reproduction A living thing can **reproduce** when it is an adult. That means it can make more living things like itself. Organisms reproduce in many different ways. But all living things make more living things. Raccoons make more raccoons. Apple trees make more apple trees.

CHECK YOUR ANSWERS ON PAGES 314-329!

make THE connection

GROWING UP

Explore how humans grow and change.

1. Make a table with two columns. Label the first column "Baby." Label the second column "Now."

2. Think about how your body has changed since you were a baby. In the "Baby" column write down what your body was like when you were born. For example, you might write "No teeth" in the first column.

3. What is your body like now? Write these things under "Now."

4. Think about the things you could do when you were a baby. Write these things under "Baby."

5. What things can you do now? Write these things under "Now."

6. You will keep changing as you become an adult. What things will you be able to do when you grow up that you can't do now?

Death Some day, all living things die. The amount of time between birth and death is called a **life span**. Some living things live for only a very short time. Mayflies are small water insects that live for less than one day. Other living things live a very long time. The oldest tree in the United States is more than 4,600 years old, and it is still growing!

Mayfly

Dead tree

These sunflowers are dying. What comes next in the sunflower cycle? If you guessed that their seeds will grow into new sunflowers, you are correct!

GO ONLINE

Movie of a plant's life cycle

www.brainpopjr.
com/science/
plants/plantlife
cycle/preview.
weml

Plant Life Cycles

Like all living things, plants have a life cycle. Some plants begin life as **spores**. Others start out as **seeds**.

Flowering plants begin life as a seed. If the seed falls onto the ground and has the right amount of sunlight and water, it begins to grow. The young plant is called a **seedling**. When the plant is an adult, it will make flowers. Plants use flowers to reproduce, or make more plants.

Corn seedlings

◉ In the life cycle of a dandelion, the young plant grows from a seed and makes flowers. The adult plant reproduces and makes seeds. The seeds are released. Then the dandelion dies.

Some flowering plants die after they make seeds. Other flowering plants do not die after they release their seeds. These plants grow new flowers and make more seeds every year. Fruit trees are an example of plants that grow new flowers each year.

These trees will make flowers and ◉ seeds many times before they die.

SEEDS   PLANT

 grass

 oak tree

 watermelon

 beans

See also:
page
96
Plants

GLaD SCiENTiST

CHECK YOUR ANSWERS,
PaGES 314-329!

HOW WiLL iT GROW?

Create your own chart of the life cycle of a tree.

1. Find the seed of a tree in your neighborhood. Glue the seed to a piece of construction paper.

2. Draw four boxes on the paper. Label the boxes "Seedling," "Young tree," "Mature tree," and "Dead tree."

3. Now draw a picture in each box that shows what you think the different stages of a tree's life looks like.

Animal Life Cycles

Animals have life cycles, too. But different types of animals go through the life cycle in different ways.

Some animals spend time growing inside the body of their mother before they are born. They get food and protection from their mother's body. Mammals, some fish, and some reptiles are born this way.

When a mammal is born, the mother gives the baby milk. Babies look like their parents, but they are still very small. A baby has a lot of growing to do before becoming an adult.

◎ Some young animals look like adults. This bear cub looks like its mother.

GO ONLINE

Ladybug Facts

www.kritter facts.com/lady bug/food-458. htm

Some young animals change their body shape when they grow. These ladybug larvae will not look like ladybugs until they become adults. ◎

Other animals hatch from eggs. The egg gives the tiny animal food and protection. When it is big enough, the young animal breaks out of the egg. Insects, birds, amphibians, some fish, and some reptiles are born this way.

See also:
page
64
Animals

A baby chick is born. It hatches from an egg. It looks like a bird. It does not look like a turtle or any other animal that hatches from an egg.

Thinking BIG™

zoom

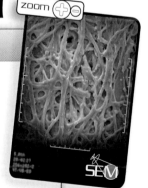

www.carolinacurriculum.com/ThinkingBig

Record your ideas in your science notebook.
- Is this a solid, a liquid, or a gas? Why do you think so?
- Write one question you have about this picture.

Solve IT

1) I feel smooth on the outside.
2) I am part of a bird's life cycle.
3) Air goes in and out of me.
4) I'm a home until I crack.
5) What am I?

Answers on pages 314–329!

Metamorphosis: Butterfly

Like many insects, butterflies change shape as they grow into adults. This is called **metamorphosis** (met uh MOR fuh suhs).

1.

⊙ The young monarch caterpillar grows in the egg for about four days.

> The life cycle of a butterfly has four stages. The butterfly looks different in each stage.

Egg An adult butterfly lays tiny, round eggs on leaves. The young butterfly will grow inside the egg before it hatches. When it hatches, the butterfly is in the form of a caterpillar.

A caterpillar ⊙ eats so much that it outgrows its skin! This monarch caterpillar will be a caterpillar for about two weeks.

2.

Caterpillar A caterpillar is a butterfly **larva**. A caterpillar hatches from its egg. Then it begins to eat leaves. A caterpillar will shed its skin four times or more as it grows larger.

Adult The chrysalis breaks open. An adult butterfly comes out! Adult butterflies can reproduce. Females lay eggs, and the life cycle starts all over again.

◉ This adult monarch butterfly has just come out of its chrysalis. It must unfold its wings and let them dry. This takes about two hours. Then it can fly.

See also:
page
64
Animals

Chrysalis The caterpillar stops eating and turns into a **chrysalis** (KRI suh luhs). It has a hard outer shell. This is the pupa stage of a caterpillar. Inside the chrysalis, the caterpillar's body changes. A new body forms.

This picture ◉ shows a monarch caterpillar changing into a chrysalis. The caterpillar will change into a butterfly inside the hard shell. This takes about ten days.

Metamorphosis: Frog

Insects are not the only animals that change shape as they grow into adults. Amphibians (am FI bee uhnz) also go through metamorphosis. **Amphibians** are animals that spend part of their life in the water and part of their life on land. A frog is an amphibian that goes through metamorphosis.

Frogs have three stages in their life cycle. The three stages are egg, tadpole, and frog. The biggest changes in a frog's body happen in the tadpole stage.

Is That a Fact?

Eating Eyes

Did you know that some frogs use their eyes to eat? The frog uses its eyeballs to help swallow! When a frog catches a fly or gets some other food in its mouth, its eyes close. The eyeballs move down into the frog's head. The eyeballs help push the food down the frog's throat.

GO ONLiNE

To learn more about frogs, check out this Web site!

• Frogs are Amphibians

http://www.kidzone.ws/lw/frogs/facts1.htm

Egg An adult frog lays many eggs at one time. The eggs do not have a hard covering, so most frogs lay eggs in water.

1.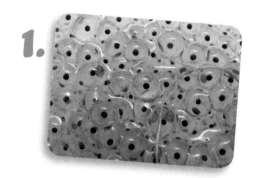

Tadpole A **tadpole** hatches from the egg. A tadpole is very small and has a head and a tail. Tadpoles also have gills. **Gills** are special structures that allow the tadpole to breathe underwater.

2.

After about six weeks, the tadpole grows back and front legs. Skin grows over the gills. Lungs begin to form. The head gets bigger. The tadpole's legs and head get larger, and the tail gets smaller and smaller.

Adult An adult frog has **lungs** instead of gills so that it can breathe on land. A frog also takes in air through its skin! It does not have a tail. It does not live in the water, but it often lives near water. When an adult frog reproduces, it lays eggs. The life cycle begins again.

3.

Ecosystems

What Is an Ecosystem?

Imagine an area with tall trees and a stream. Think about the animals and plants and the sunlight and rainfall in the area. You are imagining a forest ecosystem (EE koh sis tuhm). An **ecosystem** is made up of all of the living things and nonliving things that depend on each other in a certain area.

We divide living things in an ecosystem into groups called populations (pop yoo LAY shuhnz). A **population** is a group of the same kind of living thing that lives in an area. All of the oak trees in a forest are a population. All of the minnows in a lake are a population.

We call all of the populations in an area a **community** (kuh MYOO nuh tee). You live in a community. Your community includes people, pets, trees, flowers, and other populations.

○ This is a population of penguins. They are all the same type and live in the same area.

This community includes ◉ populations of zebras, elephants, giraffes, and trees.

An ecosystem also includes nonliving things. Water, air, soil, weather, and light are some of the nonliving things in an ecosystem.

An ecosystem has different types of habitats. A **habitat** is the place where an organism lives and gets all of the things it needs. A pond is a habitat for turtles. An ant's habitat is an ant colony.

The water, rocks, air, soil, ◉ and other nonliving things are part of this ecosystem.

◉ These squirrels' habitat is a tree in a wooded area.

Do you have a pet fish? The fish's habitat is a bowl with water and food. It might even have a special rock for the fish to swim through.

Sometimes an organism can change its habitat. Beavers build dams on rivers and streams. Birds use sticks to build nests. Even humans build houses to live in.

What Is a Habitat?

What kind of habitat does your favorite animal have? What is in that habitat? Write your answers in your science notebook.

FIND ANSWERS on 314 – 329

Types of Ecosystems

There are many ecosystems on Earth. Each ecosystem has different kinds of living and nonliving things.

Oceans Oceans are made of salt water. Only some types of organisms can live in salty water. Jellyfish, seaweed, and dolphins live in saltwater ecosystems.

This crab lives in an ocean ecosystem.

Long ears on this jackrabbit give off body heat, which helps it stay cool in the desert.

Deserts Deserts do not receive much rain. Organisms that live in the desert must be able to live without much water. They must also have ways to survive very hot days. Some animals have body parts that help them stay cool in the Sun.

See also:
page
64

Animals

The gila monster, a type of lizard, stores water in its tail.

The sagebrush plant grows in the desert. It needs lots of sunlight but very little rain.

Tundras Tundras are very cold. The ground is frozen much of the time. Tundra plants have very short growing seasons. Thick fur or feathers help some animals keep warm in the winter. Polar bears have furry feet so that they don't slip on the ice.

See also:
page
186
Weather,
Seasons,
and
Climate

Seals have layers of fat to protect them from the cold.

A toucan lives in a tropical rain forest.

Forests Forests have many large trees. One kind of forest is a **rain forest**. Rain forests are found near Earth's equator. They are very warm and wet.

Did **You** Know?

Leafcutter ants are a type of insect that live in the rain forest. They cut pieces from leaves and take them back to their nest. A fungus grows on the leaves. This fungus becomes the ants' food.

continued (125)

See also:
page
96
Plants

Another kind of forest is a **deciduous** (dih SIJ oo uhs) forest. These forests are filled with trees that lose their leaves in the fall. The weather in deciduous forests changes in summer and winter. Organisms must be able to live in both cold and warm weather. The white-tailed deer is one type of animal that lives in a deciduous forest.

SUMMER

The fur of the white-tailed deer changes to gray in winter and red in summer. This helps the deer blend in with its environment as the seasons change.

WINTER

GO ONLINE

To learn more about ecosystems, check out these Web sites!

- **Rachel Carson: Environmentalist**
  www2.scholastic.com/browse/article.
  jsp?id=4964

- **Food Webs**
  www.gould.edu.au/foodwebs/kids_web.htm

Grasslands Most of the plants in grasslands are grasses. Many grassland animals eat seeds and grass. Grasslands can be found all over Earth.

Bison live in  a grassland ecosystem.

CHECK YOUR ANSWERS ON PAGES 314-329!

WE'RE ALL IN THIS TOGETHER

Describe a community.

1. Think of a community that has many populations. An example would be a lake community. Write it down.

2. What kinds of populations live in that community? A lake community has geese, ducks, swans, cattails, fish, and water lilies.

3. Draw pictures of all the populations you can think of that live together to form that community.

Interactions in Ecosystems

Organisms in an ecosystem need other organisms. Animals depend on other living things for a place to live. Trees are homes for birds. Lakes are homes for fish.

See also:
page 88
Food Energy

Organisms also depend on each other for food. Animals eat food to get the energy they need. A **food chain** shows how organisms get their food.

A FOOD CHAIN

All food chains start with energy from the Sun. Plants use the energy in sunlight to make food.

Some energy is stored inside the plant. A deer gets this energy by eating the plant.

Then a wolf gets energy by eating the deer.

What happens if there is a change in the food chain? How does that affect the ecosystem?

Look at the food chain on the opposite page. Imagine that people kill all the wolves in the food chain. Now there are no wolves to kill and no wolves to eat the deer. The deer population grows and grows. There are not enough grass and plants for all the deer to eat. The deer population dies because there isn't enough food.

See also:
page
96
Plants

You can see that any change in a food chain can hurt the ecosystem.

Maybe you live near a park. If you do, you will probably find grass and grasshoppers there. What do you think the grasshoppers eat? And what animal eats the grasshoppers?

CHECK YOUR ANSWERS ON PAGES 314-329!

iT ALL DePeNDS

Explore the ways that living things depend on each other and their environments.

1. Think about a natural area near where you live. It could be a garden, a park, a lake, or other place.

2. What plants live in that ecosystem?

3. What animals live in that ecosystem?

4. Think about what the living things that live in that ecosystem need to eat. Then draw a simple food chain.

5. What other ways do living things in this ecosystem depend on each other?

Changes in Ecosystems

All of the living and nonliving things in an ecosystem need each other. Changes are harmful to an ecosystem. Many parts of the ecosystem can be hurt.

◉ Forest fires can be started by lightning or by humans. The fire will change the ecosystem.

Floods can kill ◉ animals and plants.

◉ Lakes dry up and trees die during a drought.

Sometimes an area might not have rain for a long time. This is called a drought (DROWT). Animals and plants might die without enough water. Some animals would have to move to another area.

Big changes in an ecosystem can harm some organisms. They might become threatened or endangered. A living thing is **threatened** if its population keeps getting smaller and smaller.

See also:
page
64
Animals

Sea turtles are animals that are threatened. Some beaches have been roped off to keep people away from the turtles' nests.

A living thing is **endangered** (in DAYN juerd) if its population is very small.

A living thing becomes **extinct** (ik STINKT) when it no longer lives anywhere. The dodo was a bird that lived a long time ago. Humans destroyed the forests where the dodos lived. They are now extinct.

The Dodo (*Didus ineptus*).

The dodo bird became extinct many years ago.

Grizzly bears are no longer endangered.

131

Earth Science

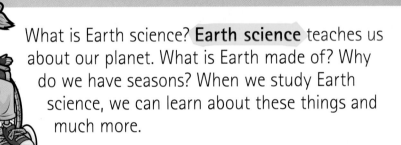

What is Earth science? **Earth science** teaches us about our planet. What is Earth made of? Why do we have seasons? When we study Earth science, we can learn about these things and much more.

Earth and Its Landforms

What Are Landforms?

Landforms are the features that exist on Earth's land. Landforms include mountains, hills, valleys, plains, and plateaus.

Mountains are the tallest landforms.

You can see for miles from a plateau.

Mountains are areas of land that rise to big heights. **Hills** are small mounds of land. **Valleys** are narrow areas of land. They are found at the bottom and between mountains or hills. **Plains** are large, flat areas of land that do not have many trees. **Plateaus** are also areas of flat land. But plateaus are areas that are higher than the land around them.

Rocks, Soil, and Water

● Rocks come in all shapes and sizes.

Rocks are hard pieces of Earth made up of minerals. They make up much of Earth's land. Rocks come in many forms, shapes, and sizes. Heat and water affect how rocks form, as well as the sizes and shapes they take.

See also: page 142

Minerals and Rocks

Soil is the top part of Earth's surface. Soil is made of tiny bits of rock and other things. Soil is the part of the land where plants can grow.

● Different plants grow in different types of soil.

Oceans make ● up more area of Earth's surface than land does.

Earth also has water on its surface. The oceans hold most of Earth's water. This seawater is very salty. Lakes, rivers, and streams have freshwater. People and land animals can drink only freshwater.

See also: page 160

Soil

Our Changing Earth: Weather, Erosion, and Glaciers

Landforms on Earth do not stay the same. The surface of Earth is always changing. Some changes happen very slowly. Others happen quickly. Sometimes we can see and feel the changes, and other times we cannot.

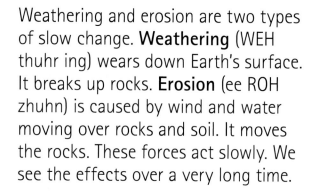

Weathering and erosion are two types of slow change. **Weathering** (WEH thuhr ing) wears down Earth's surface. It breaks up rocks. **Erosion** (ee ROH zhuhn) is caused by wind and water moving over rocks and soil. It moves the rocks. These forces act slowly. We see the effects over a very long time.

◉ Water eroded this beach.

Glaciers (GLAY shuhrz) are masses of ice that started out as snow. The snow builds up over time. The snow mounds become big ice mounds. The glaciers move slowly over the land. They change Earth's surface as they move.

Glaciers can be ◎ big and solid.

GLAD SCIENTIST

3-D LANDFORMS

You will need a shoebox, scissors, glue, and brown, green, and blue construction paper.

1. Draw mountains on the brown construction paper. Cut them out.
2. Draw hills and plateaus on the green construction paper. Cut them out.
3. Draw ocean waves or lakes on the blue construction paper. Cut them out.
4. Glue the mountains onto the inside bottom of the shoebox.
5. Glue the hills and plateaus in front of the mountains.
6. Glue the ocean waves or lakes in front of the hills and plateaus.

Our Changing Earth: Earthquakes and Volcanoes

An **earthquake** is when Earth shakes. It usually happens near a crack in Earth called a **fault**. A **volcano** is a mountain that is made from cooled lava and rock. Earthquakes and volcanoes cause fast changes in Earth's surface.

The Great San Francisco Earthquake of 1906.

Sometimes Earth trembles and shakes. The shaking can be weak or strong. Strong earthquakes can do a lot of damage to the land and to buildings.

We can measure the energy of earthquakes using the Richter scale. Earthquakes that measure less than 2.0 on the Richter scale are weak. The higher the number, the stronger the quake. No earthquake has ever measured 10.0 on the Richter scale—that's the strongest possible quake. Have you ever felt an earthquake?

Deep below the surface of Earth rocks are so hot that they melt. Melted rock is called **magma**. Lava, ash, and hot gases can burst out of cracks in the ground. Sometimes the lava cools and builds up over and over again for years. Then the buildup becomes a volcano.

Magma can be trouble. It can boil up and erupt from an opening in Earth.

Did You Know!

One Cool Thing About Hot Rocks
People can use energy from the hot magma below Earth's surface. Special energy plants called geothermal (GEE oh thur muhl) plants use heat from magma to boil water and make electricity. It's a really clean way to get power.

Natural and Manmade Resources

See also:
page
198

Natural
Resources

Earth has many natural resources. A **natural resource** is something from planet Earth that human beings can use to make things they need or want.

natural resources

what they make

Iron ore

Steel

Cotton

Clothes

Trees

Buildings

The Shasta Dam prevents the river from going out to the sea. The water now fills manmade Lake Shasta.

When people make large amounts of certain substances or materials, we call them manmade resources.

Rocks, soil, and oceans are natural, but not all landforms are natural. Some landforms are manmade. Manmade landforms are made by humans. Some hills, lakes, and other landforms have been made by humans.

Conserving Our Earth

We have learned that land has many forms. Land can be made by nature. Land can be manmade. The land changes all the time. Land affects people and people affect landforms. We need things from the land to live. But what if these things go away?

What does **conservation** (kon suhr VAY shuhn) mean? When we protect our natural resources, we conserve. We need to be careful of these resources. We need to protect the soil, the rocks, and the water. We also need to protect all living organisms.

Recycle means to use things over again. Before you throw something away, think. Can you recycle that bottle? Can you use the back of the sheet of paper?

We can all do our part to help conserve our Earth.

We can help keep Earth safe and clean. We can help the animals and plants. We can protect the land and the water. And that means we are protecting ourselves!

Minerals and Rocks

What Are Minerals and Rocks?

A **mineral** is a solid object that forms crystals. There are thousands of minerals on Earth. A **rock** is a solid object that contains two or more minerals. Rocks can be made up of two or more minerals. But minerals are not made of rocks.

Rocks come in all shapes and sizes. They are found everywhere on Earth.

See also:
page
186
Weather, Seasons, and Climate

Rocks can change. Big rocks can turn into little rocks. Rocks can move. Weather can change and move rocks. Rain can break down a rock. The rain may carry the pieces to a new location.

Rocks can have beautiful colors and shapes.

Rocks can be very small or they can be huge like mountains. A mountain is made of rock. Dust from dust storms is also made from rock.

Boulders are much bigger rocks. Boulders have a round shape.

You have probably seen gravel. **Gravel** is a loose mix of small pieces of rocks. People use gravel to cover roads and paths.

◉ You may have walked or ridden your bicycle on a gravel path.

Have you ever played in sand? **Sand** is made up of tiny pieces of rocks.

History **Makers**

Dust is a very small form of rock.

The Dust Bowl (1930s)

The Dust Bowl of the 1930s was caused by a long period with little or no rain. Topsoil was blown off fields, creating dust storms. The dust was so thick that it looked like night during the daytime. People who lived through the storms said it was like having sand thrown in their face.

...untain

Boulders **Gravel** **Dust** **Sand**

Characteristics of Minerals

Minerals have many shapes. They also have many sizes. Minerals are made of elements. Elements join in different ways to form different minerals.

Calcite is a mineral used for making glass and cement.

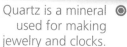

Quartz is a mineral used for making jewelry and clocks.

How many colors do you see?

Minerals can be put into groups. Some ways to group minerals are by color, luster, and hardness.

Minerals come in many colors. The chemicals in a mineral will tell its color. Some minerals have just one color. Some minerals have more than one color. Minerals are often described by their color.

Minerals can be identified by their streak. **Streak** is the color a mineral makes when it is scraped on white tile. The streak of a mineral may be different from its color.

Minerals can be grouped by their luster. **Luster** is how light is reflected off the mineral. Some minerals are dull. Some minerals are waxy. Some are glassy. And some are metallic.

A mineral, like gold or silver, can be shiny. That is its luster.

Can you name objects by their luster? A steel cabinet or bookcase may be metallic. A pool of water may look glassy. A dull mineral does not have as much shine as other minerals, such as a diamond.

Minerals can be hard or soft. The hardness is rated on a scale of one to ten. Minerals that are rated "one" are very soft. Minerals that are rated "ten" are the hardest minerals. A soft mineral can be scratched with your fingernail. Do you know the softest mineral? It is talc. It can be found in face powder. What is the hardest mineral? It is diamond.

Characteristics of Rocks

There are three basic types of rocks: sedimentary (se duh MEN tuh ree), igneous (IG nee uhs), and metamorphic (me tuh MOR fik).

Weather affects rocks. Rain and wind can make big rocks into smaller rocks. These pieces of rock are called **sedimentary rocks**. How do sedimentary rocks form? Over many years, pieces of rocks are buried in the ground. They press together. Then they harden to form sedimentary rocks.

Limestone is a type of sedimentary rock.

Marble is one type of metamorphic rock.

Which-Is-Which?

igneous   metamorphic

sedimentary

1. Which rock is formed from other rock types after being exposed to heat and pressure?
2. Which rock is made from pressed pieces of shells, plants, and animals?
3. Which rock was formed from heat that then cooled and hardened?

FIND ANSWERS ON 314 - 329

○ Cooled lava is igneous rock.

Heat affects rocks. Deep inside Earth, temperatures are very hot. Rocks can melt. Melted rock is called **magma**. If the magma flows out to the surface, it is called **lava**. When the melted rocks cool, they get hard again. Rocks that have melted, cooled, and hardened are called **igneous rocks**.

The heat deep within Earth causes pressure. Pressure squeezes existing sedimentary and igneous rocks. The heat and pressure changes these rocks. They become **metamorphic rocks**.

Did **You** Know?

Sand Blast
What happens when lightning strikes a sandy beach? The sand changes form. The lightning melts the sand, and it takes on a glassy look. The new rock is called *fulgurite*.

GLAD SCIENTIST
CHeCK YOUR ANSWERS, PAGES 314–329!

ROCK GROUP

1. Collect a bunch of rocks.
2. Sort them by their different features.
3. Keep a list of the features you discover.

Earth Is Rock

As you now know, rocks and minerals are all around us. In fact, Earth is made up of rocks.

Earth is also made of layers. There are three layers. Rocks are found in all of the layers.

The outer layer of Earth is called the **crust**. The crust is solid. It is made up of hard rocks that can change into new forms. The crust can also be soil and sand. Soil and sand are very small pieces of rock.

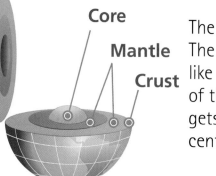

Core

Mantle

Crust

The middle layer is called the **mantle**. The top part of the mantle is solid like the crust, but the bottom part of the mantle is softer. Why? Earth gets hotter as you get closer to the center, so the heat melts the rocks.

The inside layer is called the **core**. The core has two layers, the outer core and the inner core. The outer core of Earth is hot. It is much hotter than the bottom of the mantle. Rocks in this layer are called molten rocks. Molten is another word for "melted."

You might think you would find melted rock at the inner core of Earth. But that's not correct. The rocks are solid again. There is much pressure at the center of Earth, and this pressure makes the rocks solid.

Structure and Time of Earth

How do we know so much about what makes up Earth? Geologists study it. *Geo* means "Earth." Geologists study the rocks and minerals of Earth. They can even learn about Earth's past by studying its rocks and its structure. We can learn what Earth was like billions of years ago by studying rocks and minerals today.

See also:
page
152
Fossils

Geologist at work

History Makers

Walter Alvarez (1940–present)

Walter Alvarez is an American geologist. He studies Earth and its rocks and minerals. He developed a theory about dinosaurs. Alvarez studied rocks in Earth's crust. He found iridium in the rocks. Iridium is an element from an asteroid. From his research, Alvarez knew the time period the asteroid would have hit Earth. It is the same time that the dinosaurs disappeared!

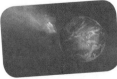

Soil

We have learned about Earth's layers. We have learned about its rocks and minerals. **Soil** is part of Earth. Soil is made up of parts of rocks, but it is so much more. Soil is also made up of living things.

○ What kinds of things live in soil? Bugs live in soil. Plants live in soil.

Without soil, plants would not survive. Food for plants is grown in soil, and rain collects in soil to keep the plants watered. If plants don't survive, humans and animals don't survive. Plants, animals, and humans all depend on soil in order to live.

Just as Earth has layers, so does soil. The top layer is called **humus** (HYOO muhs). Dead leaves and twigs can be found in this layer. The next layer is topsoil. Plants and bugs live and grow in topsoil. Below the topsoil is a layer called subsoil. It is a harder soil. Some plants and animals live here, but not as many as in the topsoil. The bottom layer is the hardest layer. It is made up mostly of rock.

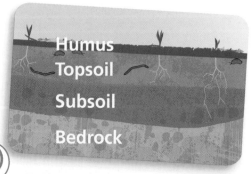

Humus

Topsoil

Subsoil

Bedrock

Trees help ○ soil. Rows of trees block the wind that might sweep away the soil. Farmers plant rows of trees to help protect the soil.

Common Uses of Minerals and Rocks

We see minerals and rocks all around us. We talked about dust and gravel. We also talked about mountains and boulders. Gold and silver are minerals. How about other forms of minerals and rocks? Can you name some?

◉ Chalk is a sedimentary rock. It is similar to limestone.

Even mud is ◉ rock. It's just not a solid rock.

Stone is used for roads and buildings. Sand and gravel are used to make bricks and pathways. Clay is used in dishes, pottery, and even kitty litter. Do you know your birthstone? Gems that make the birthstones are minerals.

◉ Stone and steel used to make bridges come from rocks.

Fossils

What Are Fossils?

Do you know what a fossil looks like? Have you ever seen a fossil? **Fossils** are the traces or remains of living things that died a long time ago. Fossils can be plants. They can be animals. The plants and animals lived a long time ago. The oldest fossils are from 3.5 billion years ago.

How are fossils made? When an animal or a plant dies, it might be buried under mud, sand, or soil. This is called **sediment**. The soft parts of the organism rot away. But sometimes the hard parts such as bones, teeth, or shells are left behind. After many years, the sediment hardens and becomes rock. The fossils can be seen in the rock.

See also:
page
142

Minerals
and Rocks

An ammonite fossil in
sedimentary rock

A fossil of a dinosaur's tail

Types of Fossils

There are different types of fossils. A **mold fossil** is an impression left in soft sediment. A **cast fossil** is made when a mold fossil is filled with minerals that harden over time.

Sometimes a fossil is not part of the animal's body. **Trace fossils** can be footprints or poop or burrows. Trace fossils tell us about the animal's environment and behavior.

◉ A fossil can be made from a whole animal, like this dragonfly.

◉ Dinosaur poop is a trace fossil.

Fossils can be found in amber. **Amber** is tree resin. It may drip and trap a bug. Over time, the resin hardens with the insect still inside.

◉ These ants were trapped in amber.

What Becomes a Fossil?

Think of things that can become a fossil. Write your answers in your science notebook.

FIND ANSWERS on 314 – 320

Where Are Fossils Found?

Fossils of Water Organisms Most people think of dinosaurs when they hear the word *fossil*. But dinosaur fossils are only a small part of all fossils. Many fossils come from sea animals. Most fossils come from animals with shells and bones because the hard parts of the animal did not rot away.

Shell fossil

Fish fossil

Fossils can be found anywhere. Most fossils are covered by sediment. Sedimentary rock is usually found near water or where water once was. This means that most fossils are from animals that lived in or near water.

One of the most common fossils is of a sea animal called an ammonite (AM uh nyt). We can see evidence of their shells. The shells protected them. The shells were hard and did not rot. Ammonites lived millions of years ago. They became extinct at the same time as the dinosaurs became extinct.

Ammonite

Fossils of Land Organisms Fossils can also be found in the desert. You probably know all about a popular desert fossil—the dinosaur. Dinosaurs didn't have shells like some animals found near water. Dinosaurs had bones.

See also: page **160**
Soil

Is That a Fact?

Never Toothless

Dinosaurs had replaceable teeth. When they lost a tooth, they would grow a new one. Sharks, alligators, and crocodiles can grow new teeth, too.

Spinosaurus (SPY nuh SAWR us) is a type of dinosaur. Their fossils show that they had spines coming from their backs. These spines might have helped the animals cool off in the heat. Their fossils are found in Africa, in the Sahara Desert. When Spinosaurus lived, the desert had a tropical climate. Spinosaurus may have played in rivers and lakes in what is now the world's biggest desert!

◉ These fossils were found in Africa.

This dinosaur fossil is ◉ embedded in rock and sand.

Prehistoric Plants and Animals

See also:
page
142

Minerals
and Rocks

What are prehistoric plants? What are prehistoric animals?
They lived when no people were around to write about
them. But fossils tell their story.

Most plant and animal life disappeared at the same time.
This time is called the Cretaceous-Tertiary
(krih TAY shuhs • TER shee air ee) Boundary, or K-T
Boundary. It happened about 65 million years ago.

Imagine you have a picture album, and all the pictures show
a little kid in a superhero cape. Every single time someone
took her picture, she had on a cape.

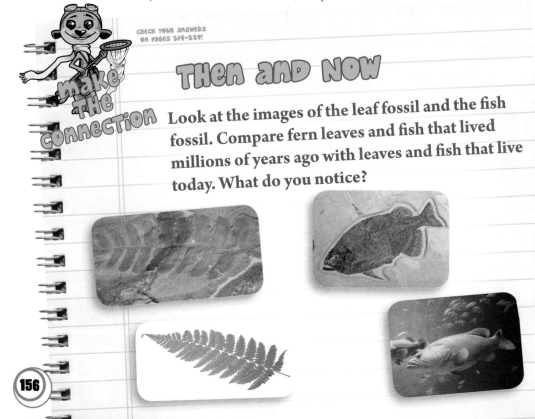

CHECK YOUR ANSWERS
ON PAGES 314-329!

make
the
connection

THEN AND NOW

Look at the images of the leaf fossil and the fish
fossil. Compare fern leaves and fish that lived
millions of years ago with leaves and fish that live
today. What do you notice?

But in newer pictures she's not wearing the cape. You can tell that something changed. (Maybe she lost the cape, or she didn't like it anymore.)

The same thing happens with fossils. Scientists find lots and lots of different kinds of fossils right up to a certain date, and then all of them almost disappear. This is a sign that almost all the organisms died at that time.

Why did most of the plants and animals die? One cause might be climate change. Cold temperatures killed many plants. Many dinosaurs ate only plants. Without the plants, the dinosaurs began to die, too.

Most scientists think that an asteroid hit Earth and threw tons of dust into the air. The climate became much too cold, and sunlight could not reach the plants.

History **Makers**

**Luis Alvarez
(1911–1988)**

Luis Alvarez and his son, Walter Alvarez, discovered an element in some Earth rocks that comes from asteroids. They believed that a big asteroid hit Earth and left this element scattered in a thin layer on the ground. This happened at the same time as the K-T Boundary, 65 million years ago. Luis and Walter Alvarez developed a theory that the asteroid explosion caused most of Earth's plants and animals to become extinct.

Digging It Up

Scientists look for fossils in many places. Remember sedimentary rock? That is where most fossils are found. **Erosion** (ee ROH zhuhn) causes rock or soil to wear down. Erosion can uncover fossils. Many fossils can be found on hills or in valleys where erosion took place.

There may be a fossil in your backyard right now!

Tyrannosaurus rex had teeth the size of bananas.

See also:
page **134**
Earth and Its Landforms

What is a paleontologist (pay lee uhn TAH luh jist)? A **paleontologist** is someone who studies prehistoric life. She studies fossils. Some paleontologists study fossils of animals. Some study plant fossils. Paleontologists learn about the history of Earth. They discover different forms of life that lived on Earth a long time ago.

This paleontologist is busy at work.

So why do we study fossils? Why do we go in search of them? Because they are cool to look at, and it's fun to look into the past. We can actually see what roamed our Earth millions of years ago.

⊙ A dinosaur left its mark on Earth.

But why should we study fossils? Fossils help scientists know how old rocks are. Fossils give us clues about what happened on Earth millions of years ago. They tell us how life changed. Fossils tell us what happened in Earth's history and when it happened.

Do you like to study fossils? Go ahead—get your hands dirty. Play in the rocks. Dig around. Peer in between the cracks. You may just find a dinosaur staring back at you!

GO ONLINE

To learn more about fossils, visit these Web sites!
- **Fossil Mysteries**
  www.sdnhm.org
- **Fossil Museum**
  www.fossilmuseum.net
- **Discovering the Prehistoric World**
  www.discoveringfossils.co.uk

Did **You** Know?

If a dinosaur had sharp teeth, it probably ate meat. If it had flat, rounded teeth, it probably ate plants.

Soil

What Is Soil?

Soil is the outer layer of Earth where plants grow. Earth is made of rocks. Rocks can break up and become tiny, loose rocks.

See also:
page
142
Minerals and Rocks

How do the rocks break up? They may just break apart with time or they may wear away. When rocks wear away by wind or rain, it is called **weathering**.

Plants grow in soil.

Tiny rocks combine with other things to make soil. The dead remains of plants and animals are part of soil. Soil also contains air and water.

◉ Rain can break up rocks. Rain and wind can move rocks to new places.

GO ONLine

Thinking **BIG**™

Look online for a micrograph of clay, fine sand, and humus: http://www.carolinacurriculum.com/ThinkingBig.

Why Is Soil Important?

Soil is important to all life. Without soil, plants would not grow. Without plants, we would have no food. We would not have fruits or vegetables to eat. Animals would have nothing to eat. Without plants, where would we get the fabrics to make our clothes? Plants make up materials to build our homes, schools, and roadways. We depend on soil.

See also: page **96** Plants

Did **You** Know?

◉ Soil provides fresh fruit and vegetables.

Many of the antibiotics that people take to help them fight infections were taken from the bacteria found in soil.

make the connection

CHECK YOUR ANSWERS on PAGES 314-329!

HOW DOES YOUR GARDEN GROW?

You will need three clear plastic cups, sand, soil, gravel, and bean seeds.

1. Put the sand in one cup. Put the soil in a second cup. Put the gravel in the third cup.

2. Plant a seed in each cup, and cover it.

3. Add water.

4. Watch your seeds grow, and record your observations.

5. Did all three seeds sprout? Which plant grew the fastest?

Types of Soil

There are different types of soil. Each type is made of different materials. Each type has different-sized particles. Each type has a different texture (TEKS chuhr). A soil's texture is its feel. Each type has a different water content.

Sand Sand particles are much smaller than gravel. Sand is coarse and dry. It is difficult for plants to live in sand. Plants that live in sand bury their roots deep. Deep roots go down to a subsoil below the sand. The roots can find more water and nutrients in the subsoil than in the sand.

◉ Millions of tiny grains of sand make up a desert.

◉ The soil on this farmland is made from silt.

Silt The particles in silt are even tinier than those of sand. Silt is gritty, but very fine. Sometimes silt can be as fine as powder. Mud is made of silt. Many plants can grow in silt. Soil with silt makes very good farmland, but silt also washes away easily. Silt can blow away in a dust storm. It can wash away in a flood.

Clay Clay soil is very dense. The particles are close together. When it is wet, you can roll clay into a ball. When clay is dry, it is very hard. Plants cannot live in clay, but clay still has an important role. Clay holds minerals that help plants grow.

◉ Clay gets slimy when it is wet.

Different soil types are found everywhere in the world. You can observe the soil where you live. Take a look outside. What type of soil do you think is around your school? What type is around your house?

Which-Is-Which?

Slimy, Slippery, Sandy Soil Name which type of soil matches the words below.

GRiTTY   **COARSE anD DRY**   **SLimY**

FIND ANSWERS ON 314 - 329

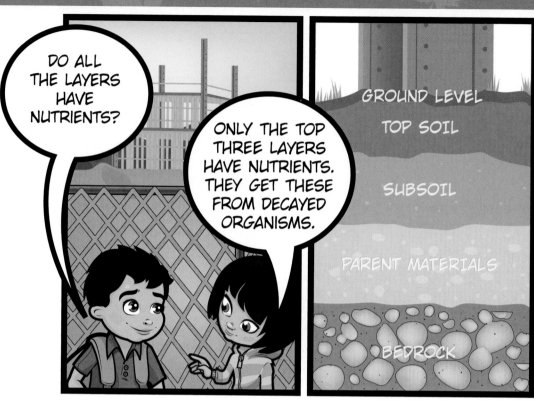

GROUND LEVEL

TOP SOIL

SUBSOIL

PARENT MATERIALS

BEDROCK

Thinking BIG™

ZOOM

www.carolinacurriculum.com/ThinkingBig

Record your ideas in your science notebook.
• Write two physical properties you see.
• How might this feel? Why?
• Might this be manmade, or found in nature? Why?

Solve IT

1) I am a solid.
2) I am so small I pour like a liquid.
3) Happy feet find me by the lake or at the ocean.
4) My best friends? Humus and clay.
5) What am I?

Answers on pages 314–329!

SEV

What Lives in Soil?

What lives in soil? The organisms (OR guh nih zuhmz) in soil are living. Most of these organisms keep the soil healthy. Healthy soil means healthy plants.

Bacteria (bak TEER ee uh) live in soil. **Bacteria** are tiny organisms with just one cell. The bacteria eat away at the dead matter causing it to rot. This process changes the dead matter to nutrients. Nutrients are good for the soil.

◉ Bacteria help keep this soil healthy.

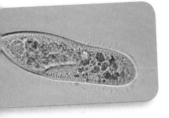

◉ Protozoa are tiny. They have only one cell.

Protozoa (proh tuh ZOH uh) live in soil. They are tiny one-celled organisms. They feed on bacteria. This process releases nitrogen into the soil. Nitrogen is a gas. Plants need nitrogen to live.

See also:
page
56

Organisms

Cupfuls of Bacteria

How much bacteria do you think live in one cup of soil? Remember, bacteria are tiny organisms. It is possible that one cup of soil can hold over six billion bacteria. That is as many bacteria as there are people on Earth!

Fungi Another organism found in soil is fungi (FUN guy). Just like bacteria, fungi help break down the dead matter and add nutrients to the soil to feed the plants.

⊙ Mushrooms are fungi.

Insects and Worms The insects that live in soil can help the soil. Earthworms play a big role in keeping soil healthy. You can think of earthworms as being construction workers in soil. As they move through the ground, they make tunnels. These tunnels allow water and air to get deeper into the soil.

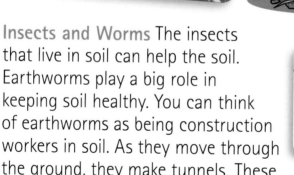

This beetle may ⊙ look scary. But some beetles are helpful beetles. They eat smaller bugs that cause disease in soil.

⊙ These earthworms are tunneling their way through the soil.

Helping Our Soil

We know how important soil is to all living things. It is important to protect it. That's not always an easy thing to do. Soil erodes. It is swept away with the rain and snow. As we continue to develop land, we use up more and more soil. So what can we do?

Composting Remember how bacteria feeds on dead matter? This process helps bring nutrients to the soil. We can help that process along by composting. **Compost** is a mixture of the decaying matter. We can create our own composts. If you set aside leaves and vegetable tops, they will someday turn into good material that can make the soil rich. Rich soil can support plants humans use for food or clothing.

Composting is nature's way of recycling.

GO ONLINE

To learn more about soil, visit these Web sites!

- **Composting**
  www.ars.usda.gov/is/kids/soil/story3/trash/htm
- **Soil Safari**
  http://school.discoveryeducation.com/schooladventures/soil/soil_safari.html

167

The Solar System

What Is in Our Solar System?

You know that Earth is a planet. But do you know what a planet is? How do the Sun and the Moon affect Earth? Are we all in the same solar system? What is a solar system?

The word *solar* means "something belonging to the Sun." A **solar system** contains the planets, moons, and other bodies in the sky that orbit around a star.

Our solar system

Our solar system contains the Sun, the Moon, and eight planets (including Earth). Asteroids and comets are also in our solar system. But most of our solar system is empty space. A model can show how small the planets are compared to the spaces between them.

Think of it this way: If the Sun were the size of a kickball, Earth would be the size of an apple seed and it would sit 24 meters (about 26 yards) away!

Stars and Telescopes

A **star** is a very hot ball of gases that is most visible at night. There are too many stars to count. Most stars are far away. They look like dots in the sky. The closer a star is to us, the brighter it seems. The Sun is the closest star to Earth. That's why it shines so brightly.

Some stars form patterns in the sky. The Big Dipper is shown here.

Telescope

Most stars are scattered across the sky, but some stars make a pattern. Star patterns stay the same over many hundreds or thousands of years.

Hubble Space Telescope

How do we know so much about space? Telescopes, radios, satellites, and rockets are just a few of the tools used to explore space. They give information to scientists back on Earth.

See also: page **178** Space Exploration

GO ONLINE

To find out more, visit these Web sites!

- **Lucy's Planet Hunt**
  http://spaceplace.nasa.gov/en/kids/spitzer/storybooks
- **NASA JPL Kids' Page**
  http://www.jpl.nasa.gov/kids/index.cfm

What Is a Planet?

A **planet** is a body in the sky that moves around a star. A planet moves in an orbit. An **orbit** is the path of one object around another object. Earth moves in an **ellipse** (ee LIPS), or a longish oval, around a star, our Sun. A planet receives its light from its star.

Earth is the fifth largest of the eight planets. It is the third planet from the Sun. It is estimated that Earth is 4.5 billion years old.

◎ This image compares the sizes of the eight planets.

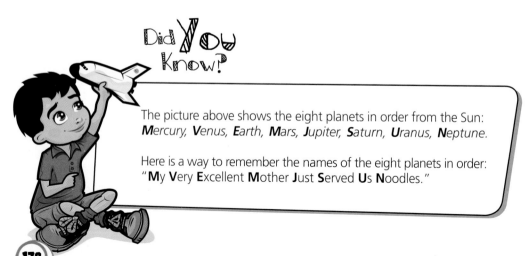

Did **You** Know?

The picture above shows the eight planets in order from the Sun: *Mercury, Venus, Earth, Mars, Jupiter, Saturn, Uranus, Neptune.*

Here is a way to remember the names of the eight planets in order: "**M**y **V**ery **E**xcellent **M**other **J**ust **S**erved **U**s **N**oodles."

Characteristics of Earth

Many types of life live on Earth. Earth has just the right temperature (TEM puhr choor) to support life. A **temperature** is how hot or how cold something is. Earth also has the right atmosphere (AT muh sfeer) for living things. The **atmosphere** is the blanket of gases that surrounds Earth.

See also:
page
142

Minerals and Rocks

Earth's atmosphere protects us from harmful radiation (ray dee AY shuhn) from the Sun. This radiation is part of the heat and energy that flows toward Earth from the Sun.

Incoming energy

Oceans cover about 70 percent of Earth's surface. The land and what lies beneath the land and oceans is rock.

This view of Earth from space shows our land and our oceans.

The Sun

The **Sun** is a star. Earth orbits around the Sun. The Sun is the largest object in our solar system.

See also:
page
238
Light

The Sun is made mostly of two gases. These are hydrogen (HEYE druh juhn) and helium (HEE lee uhm). They are the two most common gases in the universe. The rest of the Sun is made of oxygen and metals.

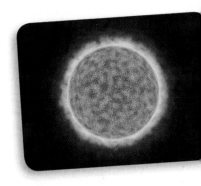

See also:
page
220
Energy

What Is the Sun Made Of?

2% Oxygen and metals

28% Helium

70% Hydrogen

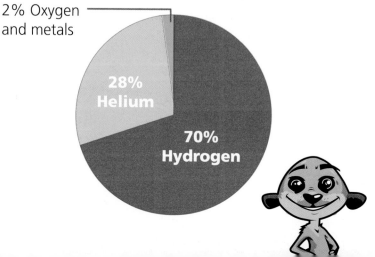

The Sun produces energy as heat and light. The heat keeps Earth's temperatures comfortable for living things. Plants need the Sun's energy to make food. Plants also provide food for other living things.

The Sun is important to the **water cycle**. The Sun warms oceans and lakes. This makes water evaporate, or change to water vapor. The water vapor mixes with cool air. The cooled water vapor condenses to form water drops. The water drops form clouds. The water drops get larger and fall to Earth as rain.

Besides Earth, seven other planets orbit the Sun. **Asteroids** (AS tuh roydz), **comets**, and other smaller objects also fall into the Sun's orbit.

◉ Eight planets orbit our Sun.

History *Makers*

Galileo Galilei (1564–1642)

Galileo invented a telescope that could magnify an object 20 times. He was able to look at the Moon and the planets. He showed that Earth and the other planets moved around the Sun. Before Galileo's discovery, people thought the Sun moved around Earth.

The Moon

Earth orbits the Sun. The Moon orbits Earth.

Like Earth, the Moon is made of rock and has three layers: a crust, a mantle, and a core. Unlike Earth, the Moon does not have an atmosphere.

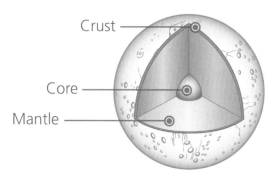

Crust

Core

Mantle

When you look at the Moon, you probably see light spots and dark spots. These are the craters on the Moon. The Moon also has a smooth side. The smooth side was caused by lava flows. Most of the Moon is covered with dust and pieces of rock. These were caused by meteor hits.

See also:
page
142
Minerals
and Rocks

Earth has a natural force that pulls objects toward it. This is called **gravity**. Earth has a gravitational (gra vih TAY shuhn uhl) pull on the Moon. The Moon has gravity, too. Its pull is weaker than Earth's pull, but it is strong enough to affect the ocean tides.

We see gravity at work when ocean waters rise and fall.

The Moon orbits around Earth once a month. You might look at the Moon each night. But does it always have the same size and shape? No. Why is that? The Moon goes through phases.

It takes 29.5 days for the Moon to circle around Earth.

The Eight Phases of the Moon

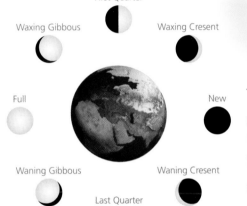

First Quarter

Waxing Gibbous

Waxing Cresent

Full

New

Waning Gibbous

Waning Cresent

Last Quarter

The Sun's light hits the Moon at different angles as the Moon orbits Earth. A **phase** is the part of the Moon we can see. Each phase has a different name.

make the connection

iT'S JUST a PHase

Record your own observations of the Moon's phases.

1. Observe the Moon each night for one month.

2. Write a description of what you see in your science notebook every night. What does the Moon look like? Where in the sky is the Moon?

3. Label the description with one of the eight phases.

4. Note how the Moon seems to travel across the sky.

More Moons

Only six of the planets have **moons**. Some moons can be seen with a telescope. Some moons can be seen only by spacecrafts exploring space. New moons are still being discovered.

Planet	Number of Known Moons	Some Names of Moons
Mercury	0	
Venus	0	
Earth	1	Moon
Mars	2	Phobos and Deimo
Jupiter	60+	Io, Europa, Ganymede, Callisto
Saturn	20+	Titan, Mimas, Rhea, Hyperion
Uranus	27	Miranda, Ariel, Titania
Neptune	13	Triton

Triton is one of Neptune's moons.

Earth has one moon.

Io and Ganymede are two of Jupiter's moons.

Space Exploration

What Is Space Exploration?

Space exploration is learning about space. It is about exploring space and everything in it. That includes planets such as Earth. It includes the Sun and the Moon. It includes the solar system and stars. We send machines to space to take pictures. We send people into space to observe and record. Space exploration is a process of discovery.

We make inventions (in VENT shuhnz) to help us get into space. These inventions help us here on Earth, too. We learn about resources in space that teach us how to use resources on Earth. Space exploration is endless.

See also:
page
168
The Solar System

Did You Know?

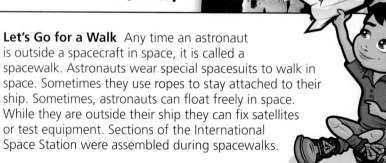

Let's Go for a Walk Any time an astronaut is outside a spacecraft in space, it is called a spacewalk. Astronauts wear special spacesuits to walk in space. Sometimes they use ropes to stay attached to their ship. Sometimes, astronauts can float freely in space. While they are outside their ship they can fix satellites or test equipment. Sections of the International Space Station were assembled during spacewalks.

Satellites

A **satellite** (SAT uh lyt) is an object that orbits a planet. The first satellite to orbit Earth was *Sputnik 1*. It was a Russian satellite. It launched in 1957.

Sputnik 1 carried radios. They sent signals to Earth. The space team listened to the signals. They gathered facts. They learned about Earth's atmosphere.

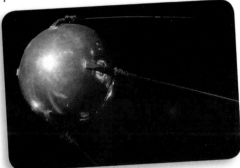

Americans sent *Vanguard 1* to space in 1958. *Vanguard 1* went higher than all other satellites. It was powered by the Sun. Radios on board sent information to Earth. Radio contact was lost in 1964. So what happened to *Vanguard 1*? It's still in space! It has been orbiting Earth for more than 50 years!

◉ Counting its antennae, *Sputnik 1* was 112 inches long and weighed 184 pounds.

Satellites are still sent into space. The satellites already in space continue to send information. Some tell us about Earth. Others look out into space.

◉ Radios on satellites send signals to Earth. The signals transmit information.

Manned Moon Missions

When did the first humans land on the Moon? It was July 20, 1969. The name of the mission was Apollo 11.

The goal of the mission was to land on the Moon and return to Earth safely. The astronauts did much more. They brought back samples from the Moon. The samples were rocks. The rocks were 3.7 billion years old. These samples were the first to come from another planetary body.

● The U.S. Postal Service issued this stamp in honor of Neil Armstrong, the first person to set foot on the Moon.

● The Moon has a rocky, dusty surface.

 History *Makers*

Lunar Landing

On July 20, 1969, Apollo 11 landed on the Moon. The astronaut Neil Armstrong was the first person to walk on the Moon. His famous words as he stepped on the Moon's surface were, "That's one small step for man, one giant leap for mankind."

There is no wind on the Moon. The American flag on the Moon has a crossbar through the top of the flag so that it appears to be flying.

See also:
page
142
Minerals
and Rocks

Unmanned Mars Missions

To this date, no astronaut has walked on Mars, but we have sent unmanned missions to Mars. Many countries have had unmanned Mars missions. The goal of the missions is to find out what Mars is like. What is it made of? What is its temperature? How old is it?

See also:
page
186

Weather, Seasons, and Climate

Humans could not breathe on Mars. The atmosphere is too thin.

We have learned that the water on Mars disappeared. There are empty stream beds on Mars. We have learned that Mars has canyons and ice caps, just like Earth. Mars has an atmosphere, but it is very thin. The atmosphere is very dusty. It is also very cold.

Did You Know?

One Mars rover was named by a kid! The rover *Sojourner* needed a name. A contest was held for students. They were asked to name a heroine. Students wrote an essay about how the accomplishments of their heroine related to a Mars mission. The winner was 12-year-old Valerie Ambroise. Her heroine was Sojourner Truth. Sojourner Truth was an African-American who lived in the Civil War. She traveled the country promoting freedom and rights for all people. The name "Sojourner" means traveler, a good name for the Mars rover.

Inhabited Space Stations

An inhabited space station is a space station where people live. These space stations orbit Earth.

The first long-term space station was Mir. Mir was launched by the Soviet Union. It was in space for almost ten years.

The United States and 16 other countries joined together to build the International Space Station. The first part of the space station was launched in 1998.

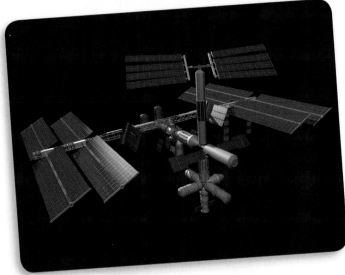

⦿ The International Space Station has been in orbit for more than ten years.

⦿ Skylab was the first U.S. space station. It was visited by three crews. The U.S. Postal Service issued this stamp in its honor.

Space Junk

Junk is stuff that is no longer needed. Did you know that there is junk in space? Pieces of space vessels or satellites sometimes come off. What happens to these pieces? They stay in orbit. And this junk doesn't just sit around! It flies around. Some of it flies more than 27,300 kilometers (17,000 miles) per hour.

What do we learn from inhabited space stations? The crew studies the environment and Earth's weather. It studies the human body in space. The crew studies elements. Crystals grown in space are used in medical research. The crew studies space flight and space living.

◉ These crystals were grown in space to help medical research.

◉ The space shuttle transports astronauts and supplies to the International Space Station.

Space Technology

In order to explore space, we have had to develop new inventions and technology. Space exploration requires many special new tools and machines. But all these tools don't only go out into space. Some of them are used right here on Earth.

Scientists work hard to prepare for space missions. Engineers and designers come up with ideas for new tools. Some of these tools have found their way into our everyday world. Take a look at this list. These items were invented to help with space exploration.

- cell phones
- lasers
- GPS systems
- pacemakers

- dehydrated food
- fire-safe clothing
- global weather satellites
- satellite television

We use these items every day without even thinking about why they were invented.

WHAT DO ASTRONAUTS EAT IN SPACE?

WE ENJOY CEREAL, SCRAMBLED EGGS, AND MAC AND CHEESE. MUCH OF OUR FOOD IS DRY, SO WE ADD WATER TO OUR MEALS JUST BEFORE WE EAT THEM.

WHY DO RONAUTS WEAR CESUITS?

SPACE CAN BE VERY COLD OR VERY HOT AND THERE IS NO OXYGEN TO BREATHE. SPACESUITS PROTECT ASTRONAUTS FROM EXTREME TEMPERATURES. THEY ALSO PROVIDE AIR FOR ASTRONAUTS TO BREATHE.

You don't have to fly to the Moon to be a space explorer. Many scientists work in labs. Many work in the field. Who knows what is yet to be discovered and what inventions will lead to new discoveries.

GO ONLINE

To learn more about exploring space, check out these Web sites!

- **Space Place**
  http://spaceplace.jpl.nasa.gov/en/kids/live/index.shtml
- **Alien Safari**
  http://solarsystem.nasa.gov/kids/index.cfm

Weather, Seasons, and Climate

What Is Weather?

Weather is what the air is doing outside. It can change from day to day. It can even change from hour to hour. It can be sunny in the morning and raining in the afternoon. Weather includes temperature, wind, cloud cover, and precipitation (pri si puh TAY shuhn). Precipitation includes rain, snow, sleet, and hail.

See also:
page
168
The
Solar
System

Which-Is-Which?

How do you dress for your weather?

FIND ANSWERS ON 314 – 329

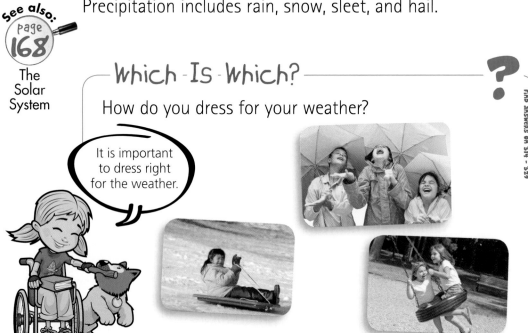

It is important to dress right for the weather.

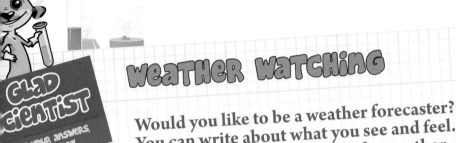

CHECK YOUR ANSWERS,
PAGES 314-329!

WEATHER WATCHING

Would you like to be a weather forecaster?
You can write about what you see and feel.
Every day, for one week, observe the weather.
Copy the following table in your Science Notebook.

1. **Temperature:** Use a thermometer if you have one. If not, write how hot or cold it seems to you. For each day, write if it feels "warmer" or "cooler" or "the same" as the day before.

2. **Wind:** Use a compass if you have one. If not, stand in front of your home. Find out the direction you are facing. Remember that direction. Every day observe the wind. Which direction is it coming from? Does it seem fast or slow? Record what you feel.

3. **Clouds:** Observe any clouds that you see. Write down what type of clouds they are.

4. **Precipitation:** Observe and record any precipitation. Is it raining? snowing? sleeting?

5. Write a report on the week's weather. How did it change? Did it stay the same? What did you find interesting?

	Temperature	Wind	Clouds	Precipitation
Monday				
Tuesday				
Wednesday				
Thursday				
Friday				
Saturday				
Sunday				

187

Weather Patterns

A **pattern** is something that is repeated over and over again. A **weather pattern** is weather that repeats over and over again. It is helpful to recognize weather patterns. They can help weather forecasters predict what the weather will be like during a certain time of the year. People can be prepared for sunny days or snowstorms.

Certain patterns might predict a storm or a flood. This information is helpful to farmers so that they can protect their crops. Other patterns might predict a long period without rain. So farmers would have to water their fields more.

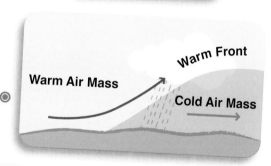

◉ Weather patterns can predict flooding or dry weather.

A **warm front** is warm air moving over colder air. It usually produces light rain or fog.

Warm fronts and cold ◉ fronts are weather patterns, too.

Warm Air Mass
Warm Front
Cold Air Mass

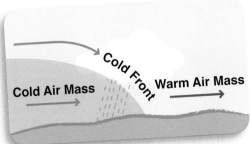

Cold Air Mass
Cold Front
Warm Air Mass

A **cold front** is cold air replacing warmer air. It brings strong thunderstorms and cooler weather.

Can We Measure Weather?

Temperature (TEM per choor) is how hot or how cold something is. Temperature is measured in degrees on a scale. The scale we use most often in the United States is the Fahrenheit (°F) scale.

A thermometer (ther MAH muh ter) measures temperature. Thermometers measure water temperature and air temperature. This type of measurement helps us predict the weather.

What is the temperature outside? The outside temperature is part of weather.

Precipitation is falling water. Rain and snow are precipitation. Precipitation falls when air moves up. As air moves up it cools. As it cools it forms little droplets. These droplets become precipitation.

Precipitation is measured using a rain gauge or a snow gauge. They measure precipitation over a set period of time. Rain and snow are usually measured in inches.

A rain gauge measures precipitation.

What is the weather like on a windy day? The air may swirl around you. It may blow you in one direction or another. Maybe it's just a slight breeze. Wind has both direction and speed. Wind speed and wind direction can be measured.

A wind vane shows wind direction. The wind turns the vane. The arrow points to the direction the wind is coming from.

Wind is the movement of air. Why does the air move? Energy from the Sun warms the land, air, and water. This makes the air temperature unequal. Unequal temperatures make the air move around. The air movement causes wind.

Wind speed is how fast the air is moving. It is measured in miles per hour. A tool called an **anemometer** (a nuh MAH muh ter) can measure wind direction and wind speed. The anemometer has a vane to measure wind direction and a shaft to measure wind speed.

When the wind spins the cups on the anemometer, you can measure the wind speed.

THE WEEK'S WEATHER

Sunday	Monday	Tuesday	Wednesday	Thursday	Friday	Saturday
68°F.	62°F.	59°F.	60°F.	56°F.	58°F.	63°F.

Weather Events

A **thunderstorm** occurs when warm air rises quickly. Energy is released in lightning and thunder. Heavy rain and sometimes hail falls. Winds are usually strong.

Lightning is an electric current. The electric charge is caused by little pieces of ice high up in the atmosphere. In a thundercloud the pieces of ice bump into each other. This makes the electric charge.

Lightning causes thunder. Lightning heats the air around it. The heated air expands and creates a sound wave. This makes the sound we know as thunder.

A **tornado** (tor NAY doh) is a storm with great force. Rotating air can create funnel clouds. If funnel clouds touch the ground, they are called tornadoes. Wind speeds in tornadoes can reach 480 kilometers (300 miles) per hour.

A **hurricane** (HUHR uh kayn) is a huge storm. It forms over warm ocean water. The warm water makes the hurricane stronger and more powerful. The strong winds and rain can damage trees and buildings.

Hurricanes can reach up to 965 kilometers (600 miles) across. Wind swirls at speeds of 120 to 320 kilometers (75 to 200 miles) per hour.

GLAD SCIENTIST

TWISTING TORNADOES

You can create your own mini tornado.
You will need:

- two empty 2-liter plastic soda bottles, labels removed
- tornado tube connector OR the two caps to the bottles with one 3/8-inch hole drilled in the center of each
- duct tape

1. Fasten the caps together, back to back, with duct tape.
2. Fill the first bottle 2/3 full with water. Attach the caps to this bottle.
3. Attach the empty bottle to the caps (opposite direction of the first bottle).
4. Turn the bottles so that the bottle with water is on top. Do not tilt it.
5. Shake the upper bottle in a circular motion.
6. Watch the tornado!

193

The Changing Seasons

Each season has its own type of weather.

A **season** is a period of the year that has a particular type of weather. There are four seasons. They are spring, summer, fall, and winter. Why do the seasons change? Earth revolves around the Sun. Earth also rotates on an axis. These changes bring the change in seasons. The weather in each season varies. It depends on where you live on Earth.

In the spring, days are longer. The temperature rises. People plant seeds in their gardens. Animals that have spent winter in places with warmer weather return. Some baby animals are born in the spring.

A newborn lamb and planting a garden are signs of spring.

Corn on the cob is a summer treat. Roses bloom in the summer.

Days are even longer in the summer. Earth is tilted toward the Sun. The temperature gets hotter. Plants are in full bloom. Many vegetables are ready to eat.

194

Earth tilts away from the Sun in the fall. The days become shorter. Temperatures are cooler. The late season vegetables are ready to eat. Animal **migration** (my GRAY shuhn) is a sign of fall. Migration means that some animals travel to warmer weather for the winter.

See also:
page #
The Solar System

See also:
page 64
Animals

Leaves change color in the fall. Monarch butterflies fly south in the fall.

The days are the shortest in the winter. Earth is tilted away from the Sun. The temperatures are cold. Only certain types of plants grow. Some animals have a long rest in the winter. This is called **hibernation** (hy buhr NAY shuhn). Their heart rate and breathing slow down to save energy.

Evergreen trees stay green in the winter. Groundhogs hibernate for the winter.

GO ONLINE

To learn more about weather, seasons, and climate, check out these Web sites!

- **Hurricanes**
  http://www.fema.gov/kids/hurr.htm
- **Weather Watching**
  http://eo.ucar.edu/webweather/
- **Everything Weather**
  http://www.weatherwizkids.com/

What Are Clouds?

A **cloud** is a large cluster of very tiny drops of water. Have you ever walked outside on a foggy day? Then you have walked through a cloud. **Fog** is a cloud that has formed closer to the ground rather than up in the sky. There are different types of clouds.

Cumulus clouds look like puffy cotton balls. They might be seen on a sunny day.

Cirrus clouds are thin and wispy. They usually form on a pleasant day.

Stratus clouds are low clouds that look like fog. They can produce a light rain or mist.

When cumulus clouds grow bigger and fill with water, they become **cumulonimbus clouds**. They usually mean a rainstorm is expected.

What Is Climate?

Climate is the weather in a particular region of the world. The climate of a region is determined after many years of watching the region's weather. It includes temperature, wind, and precipitation, but the climate does not change from day to day.

Climate changes with the seasons. A season may be warmer or cooler. It may be more or less rainy. It may be more or less sunny or cloudy. For example, the climate near the equator is hot. The climate at the North Pole is cold.

Is That a Fact?

Southern Hemisphere

What are the seasons in the Southern Hemisphere? They have the same names. But while it is summer in the Northern Hemisphere, it is winter in the Southern Hemisphere.

What is the climate in the summer where you live? How about the winter? What is your favorite climate? Your favorite season? Keep a journal of how you feel as the weather changes.

The Equator is an imaginary line. It divides the Northern Hemisphere and the Southern Hemisphere.

Natural Resources

What Are Natural Resources?

People chop down trees to make paper. We burn gas to heat houses. We dam water in rivers to make electricity. Trees, gas, and water are all natural resources!

A **natural resource** is any material that comes from nature. All the things we build are made from natural resources. All of the energy we use comes from natural resources. We are part of nature. Everything in our lives comes from nature, too. Natural resources are either renewable or nonrenewable.

Is That a Fact?

Solar Power!

Earth's most important resource is the Sun. It supplies the heat and energy that makes living on Earth possible. Every day, it gives us an amazing amount of energy. In just one hour, the Sun sends Earth more energy than humans use in an entire year!

Water, trees, and coal are examples of natural resources.

Renewable Resources At a lumber mill, tree trunks are cut into boards. A tree can be chopped down only once, but more trees can be planted. If we are careful, we will not run out of trees. They are a renewable resource.

Renewable resources do not run out. Energy from the Sun or wind is renewable. We cannot use up their supplies. The Sun will be shining on Earth for billions of years. The wind always blows somewhere. Both wind and sunshine always come back.

Nonrenewable Resources A car's tank is filled with gas. The car burns the gas to move from place to place. The gas that was burned up is gone. The tank needs to be filled again. Gas is a **fossil fuel**. Unlike trees, we cannot grow or make more fossil fuels. They are a nonrenewable resource. Once we use them all, they are gone forever.

Which-Is-Which?

WATER **COAL** **SUNSHINE** **WIND**

Label each resource as *renewable* or *nonrenewable*. Write your answers in your science notebook.

FIND ANSWERS ON 314 – 329

Material Resources

Material resources are natural resources used to make the things we use. Books are made of paper that came from trees. A concrete sidewalk is made with rocks taken from the ground. Bread is made from wheat that was grown on a farm. Almost everything you use or eat is a **material resource**.

Pencils and paper are made from trees.

Crude oil is used to make gasoline. It is also used to make plastic.

Rocks and metals are mined from the ground.

Name That Material!

GLaD SCIENTIST
CHECK YOUR ANSWERS, PAGES 314–329!

Look at the objects around you. What materials were used to make them?

1. Make a chart with four columns. The title of the columns should be "Tree," "Rock," "Metal," and "Fossil Fuel."
2. Find things in the room that are made from each material. List them in the chart.
3. Was anything made from more than one material? Which materials are renewable? Which ones are not?

Energy Resources

See also:
page
238
Light

Energy lights our homes, schools, and workplaces. It moves trucks, buses, and cars down the road. It powers our televisions and computers. It helps us cook, clean, and keep warm.

Much of our energy comes from fossil fuels like coal, crude oil, and natural gas. Coal is burned in power plants to make electricity. Crude oil is made into gasoline and jet fuel. It is also burned to heat some homes. Natural gas is burned for heat and for cooking.

This stove ◉ uses natural gas for cooking.

Other types of energy include water, wind, and the Sun. The pushing force of a river can be used to make electricity. The spinning blades of a wind turbine can make electricity, too. Solar panels get energy from sunshine.

◉ The solar panels on this house use the Sun to make electricity.

See also:
page
220
Energy

Did **YOU** Know?

Easy, Breezy Power! Wind power might seem like a new idea, but it has been used for a long time. Ancient Egyptians used wind to sail boats. The first windmills were built 1,000 years ago in Persia.

Nature's Cycles

We recycle paper, metal, and plastic. They get smashed, shredded, and reshaped to make new things. Earth recycles as well. Water, rocks, and gases change as they move around the planet.

Is That a Fact?

Water, Water Everywhere

Earth is very wet. Oceans cover much of our planet. Having enough water should not be a problem, right? Nearly all of Earth's water is salt water. Most plants and animals, including humans, need freshwater. Only a very small amount of Earth's water is freshwater, and most of it is frozen. Only 1 percent of Earth's water is both fresh and unfrozen!

The Water Cycle
Earth's water is always on the move.

① Water falls from clouds as rain, snow, sleet, or hail.

② When rain hits the ground, it sinks into the ground or it flows into rivers and streams. Rivers move water to the seas and oceans.

③ The Sun heats the oceans, and some water evaporates. Water moves through the air and forms clouds.

④ When the clouds get heavy, the water becomes liquid again and falls as rain.

The cycle begins again!

continued

The Rock Cycle Rocks go through physical changes. Deep underground it is so hot that rocks melt. **Metamorphic** (met uh MOR fik) **rocks** are formed there. Liquid, molten rock is called **magma**. Magma that flows out of volcanoes is called **lava**. Magma on or near Earth's surface cools and hardens into rock. This is called **igneous** (IG nee uhs) **rock**.

Erosion (ee ROH zhuhn) is when rain, snow, ice, or wind breaks rocks into smaller pieces. The pieces flow down rivers and streams. Slowly, these rocks become buried under more rocks. These become **sedimentary** (se duh MEN tuh ree) **rocks**. After many years, they end up deep underground again. They melt to magma, and the cycle starts again!

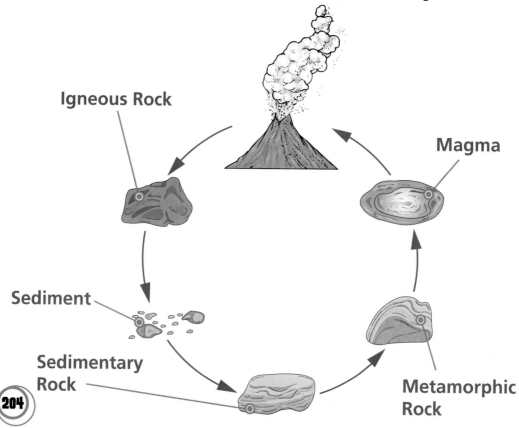

Igneous Rock

Magma

Sediment

Sedimentary Rock

Metamorphic Rock

How We Use Natural Resources

Natural resources have many uses. Soil is used to grow plants for food. Water is needed for drinking. Rocks are used to build roads, sidewalks, and buildings.

Natural Resource	Uses

Dirt, mud, and clay can be mixed with straw to build an adobe house.

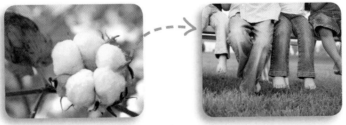

Cotton from plants can be used to make clothes.

Cows give milk, which can be made into ice cream.

Pollution

You see it when garbage has blown against a fence. You smell it when a smoky truck rolls down the street. You even hear it when the city is so loud you cannot think. **Pollution** is part of our lives. It hurts natural resources. It can also harm living things, including us.

Boxes, cans, uneaten food, old cars, and broken toys are a small sample of the things we throw away. Most garbage goes to landfills where it is buried. Litter is garbage that does not make it to the landfill. Instead, it pollutes parks, streets, rivers, and many other places.

Water and air pollution can make us sick. Water is polluted by sewage. Sewage is water that gets dumped down drains. It can be human waste, soap, old food, or chemicals. We have to clean the water we drink to be sure it is not polluted.

Air pollution is anything in the air we do not want to breathe. It can make you cough or feel sick.

If you want to make the world a cleaner place, there are ways to help.

⊙ Form a clean-up crew with an adult's help. Visit a park, and pick up litter.

⊙ Most electricity is made by burning coal. Replace at least one regular light bulb in your home with a compact fluorescent (CFL) bulb. CFLs last ten times longer, and they use a lot less energy.

⊙ Energy is used to clean our water. Wasting it wastes resources. Take shorter showers. Turn the water off while you brush your teeth.

⊙ Gas-powered cars add to air pollution. Walk or ride your bike whenever possible.

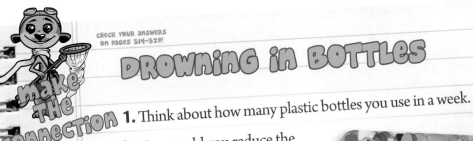

make the connection

CHECK YOUR ANSWERS
ON PAGES 314-329!

DROWNING IN BOTTLES

1. Think about how many plastic bottles you use in a week.

2. How could you reduce the number of bottles you use each week? Write down your ideas in your science notebook.

Learn the three Rs:
Reduce, Reuse, and Recycle

✳ Reduce what you use every day. It saves resources and means fewer things end up in landfills.

✳ Reuse things. This saves resources, too. Take old plastic bags to the store with you. Use egg cartons to hold paints. Draw on the back of used printer paper.

✳ Recycle paper, cans, and plastic as often as you can. Buy used clothes. Borrow books from the library.

Physical Science

What is physical science? **Physical science** explains how things work. Do you wonder why magnets and lights and seesaws work the way they do? Good! This part of the book is for you!

Matter

What Is Matter?

Matter is anything that takes up space. A piece of paper is matter. So is a rock. The air around you is matter. Even animals and plants are matter. So are people!

Long ago, people thought matter was a mixture of four basic things. They were called earth, wind, fire, and water. Now we know that this is not true.

Matter is actually made up of atoms. Atoms are the building blocks of all matter. They are very small. Atoms are so small that you cannot see them. A stack of 100,000 atoms is as thin as paper!

Flowers and butterflies are matter. Even the air in a balloon is matter.

Physical Properties

Imagine that you have found a rock that you
think might be gold. How will you know for sure?
The rock is yellow. The rock is shiny. Color and
shininess are physical properties of gold.
A **physical property** is something that you can tell
about matter without changing what that matter is.
Physical properties describe matter.

◉ The gold nugget is yellow and shiny. So is the gold ring. They have the same physical properties.

How can you describe matter?

- ◉ **Round**
- ◉ **Hard**
- ◉ **Magnetic**
- ◉ **Shiny**

- ◉ **Smooth**
- ◉ **Rough**
- ◉ **Sticky**
- ◉ **Oily**

- ◉ **Wet**
- ◉ **Hot**
- ◉ **Dry**
- ◉ **Stretchy**

make the connection

CHECK YOUR ANSWERS ON PAGES 314-329!

WILL IT FLOAT?

Use physical properties to compare and predict.

1. Compare a cork, a birthday candle, a toothpick, and a rubber stopper. How are they alike? How are they different?
2. Predict what will happen when you put them in water. Which ones will float?
3. Place them in a tub of water. Which ones floated? Which ones sank?
4. What does this information tell you?

213

Mass, Volume, and Temperature

Mass, volume, and temperature are some physical properties that can be measured.

Physical Properties

MASS

Mass is a measure of how much matter there is. Use a balance to find mass.

VOLUME

Volume is a measure of how much space something takes up. Use a graduated cylinder to find volume.

TEMPERATURE

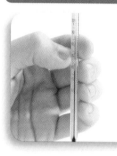

Temperature is a measure of how hot or cold something is. Use a thermometer to find temperature.

Physical Changes

What happens when you put a block of wood in water? It floats. Now, saw the block in half. Will the two pieces float? Of course they will. Even if you chop the block into very small bits, the bits will float. The wood is still wood no matter how small it is. Chopping does not change what it is. That's because chopping is a physical change.

A **physical change** is a change in matter that does not change the type of matter that it is. Other physical changes are bending, mixing, and melting.

You can **break** glass. You can **melt** glass. Both are physical changes. The glass is still glass.

breaking

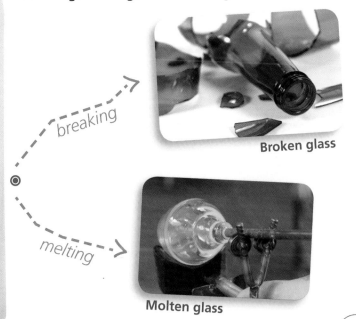

Broken glass

melting

Molten glass

States of Matter

You know that water doesn't always look the same. Sometimes you can pour it. When it forms ice, it is cold and hard. When you heat it in a kettle, it will become a cloud of hot steam. The water is still water. It is just water in a different state. State is a physical property. The **state of matter** describes if a material is a solid, a liquid, or a gas.

liquid

A **liquid** can be poured from one container to another. It takes the shape of the container that it is in.

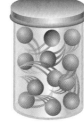

gas

Water in the air is a **gas**. It can flow like air, which is also a gas. A gas will spread out and fill the entire container that it is in.

solid

An ice cube is a **solid**. A solid keeps its shape, even when it moves from one place to another.

Is That a Fact?

Three States All At Once

Water is the only thing found in nature as all three states of matter.

Change of State

Matter can change from one state to another. This is called a **change of state**. Often, a change in temperature makes matter change its state.

ADD HEAT

TAKE AWAY HEAT

Solid to Liquid
melting
ice ---> water
rocks ---> magma

Gas to Liquid
condensing
water vapor ---> water

Liquid to Gas
vaporizing
water ---> water vapor
wet paint ---> dry paint

Liquid to Solid
freezing
water ---> ice
lava ---> rocks

Mixtures

What happens when you mix water and soil? You get mud! Mud is a mixture. A **mixture** is a combination of two or more kinds of matter.

◉ Oil and vinegar do not mix well. You have to stir the mixture before you use it on your salad.

Science Notebook

Can you mix:

1. Solids and liquids?
Yes: powdered lemonade mix and water

2. Liquids and liquids?
Yes: cranberry juice and grape juice

3. A gas and a liquid?
Yes: carbon dioxide gas and water make soda water

4. Solids and solids?
Yes: lettuce and tomatoes in a salad.

Separating Mixtures

You can use physical properties to separate mixtures. A salad is a mixture. If you do not want to eat olives, you can pick them out. They are easy to tell apart from the other things in the salad.

A magnet can be used to separate some mixtures. A magnet can separate steel cans from aluminum cans at a recycling center. Steel cans will stick to the magnet. Aluminum cans will not.

◉ Lots of foods are mixtures. You can pick parts of the mixture out by their color, shape, or size.

steel

aluminum

GLaD SCieNTiST

check your answers, pages 314-329!

FiX THe MiX

Use what you know about physical properties to separate a mixture.

1. Look at a mixture of nails, toothpicks, and plastic mixers. Would you use shape to separate this mixture? Why or why not?
2. Think of a way to separate the nails from the mixture. What will a nail stick to that wood and plastic will not?
3. How could you use water to pull out the toothpicks? What will happen to the mixture when you add water?
4. Separate the mixture. Describe the physical properties that you used to separate them.

Energy

What Is Energy?

Energy is everywhere. You can turn the pages of this book because of energy. You can see and hear what is going on around you because of energy. Energy makes trees grow. It makes volcanoes erupt. It makes Earth orbit the Sun. Energy powers it all!

Energy is what makes things move or change. There are many kinds of energy:

See also:
page
228
Sound

- Sound is energy. It moves through the air and into your ears.

- Light is energy. Light moves through the a and allows us to see

- Energy makes things move. You need energy to run.

- Energy makes matter change. Heat energy made this icy popsicle turn to liquid.

- The energy of a volcano comes from deep inside Earth.

Energy Can Change

Energy makes things change. Energy changes, too! One kind of energy can turn into another kind of energy. A lamp uses **electrical** (i LEK trik uhl) **energy**. This energy turns into light and heat. A stove uses the energy stored in natural gas. The gas energy becomes heat and light energy.

◉ This dam turns the moving energy of a river into electricity.

A car engine turns the energy ◉ in gasoline into motion.

GLAD SCIENTIST

check your answers, pages 314-329

YOU CAN'T BEAT ENERGY!

Use a drum and drumsticks to explore energy on the move.

1. Hit the drum softly. Then hit the drum harder. How are the two sounds different? Why did the sound change when you hit the drum harder? Use the word "energy" in your answer.
2. Place the end of one drumstick on the drum. Then hit the middle of the stick with the other drumstick. What do you hear? How is this an example of energy moving or changing?

Mechanical Energy

Energy can be stored or used. Stored energy is called **potential** (po TEN shul) **energy**. Energy in motion is called **kinetic** (ki NET ik) **energy**. Both kinds of energy are **mechanical** (muh KAN ih kul) **energy**.

Things in motion have energy.

◉ Any matter in motion has energy.

A battery has stored energy. Hold a battery in your hand. You will not feel any energy. Put the battery into a flashlight. Push the switch. Now the energy is in motion. It turns into electricity. Electricity turns into light energy.

See also:
page
88
Food
Energy

A battery stores energy. ◉
The flashlight uses energy.

◉ Food has stored energy. Your body turns food into energy it can use.

Energy, Motion and Force

Forces can change energy. A **force** makes things start or stop moving. A force pushes or pulls.

◉ Your breath can be a force.

When a tennis ball ◉ hits a racket, the ball moves away. Force changes the direction of the ball.

Is That a Fact?

As the World Spins

We are all in motion all the time, just by being on Earth! Earth spins at about 1,670 kilometers (1,000 miles) per hour. We are all speeding right along with it. Earth also orbits the Sun at an amazing pace: 107,000 kilometers (67,000) miles per hour!

Gravity is a special kind of force. It works only one way. Gravity always pulls things down toward the center of Earth. Gravity can change stored energy into moving energy.

See also: page **248** Motion and Forces

◉ When the sled is at the top of the hill it has potential energy. When the sled is sliding downhill it has kinetic energy.

Energy from the Sun

What does most energy on Earth come from? Gasoline? Coal? Wind? Without a doubt, it comes from the Sun. The Sun bathes Earth in light and heat. Without it, life would not be possible. Heat from the Sun keeps Earth from being a frozen wasteland. Energy in sunlight helps plants grow.

See also:
page
88
Food
Energy

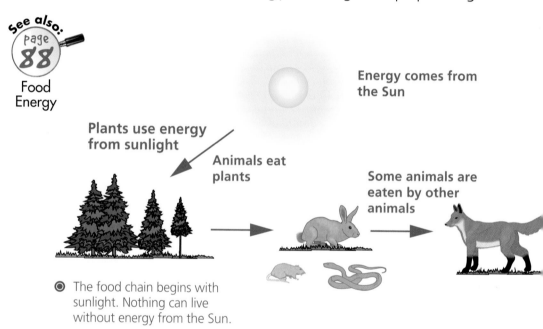

Energy comes from the Sun

Plants use energy from sunlight

Animals eat plants

Some animals are eaten by other animals

◉ The food chain begins with sunlight. Nothing can live without energy from the Sun.

See also:
page
238
Light

Energy from the Sun comes to Earth as sunlight. Light energy makes atoms more active. Matter that receives sunlight will gain heat energy.

make THE connection

CHECK YOUR ANSWERS
ON PAGES 514-529!

FUN IN THE SUN!

Use thermometers and cloth to learn about heat energy from the sun.

1. Wait for a sunny day. Lay three thermometers outside. Put them on a flat surface. Label the thermometers 1, 2, and 3. Wait until they all reach the same temperature.

2. Do not cover the bulb of thermometer #1.

3. Place a black cloth over the bulb of thermometer #2.

4. Place a white cloth over the bulb of thermometer #3.

5. Let them sit in the sun. Wait for at least two hours. What do you think will happen?

6. Write down the three temperatures in your science notebook. Are all temperatures the same?

7. Can you explain what happened? Put your answer in your science notebook.

◉ People who live and work in the desert often wear light-colored clothing. Light colors reflect heat and sunlight.

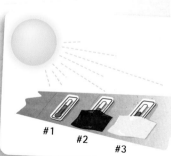

#1 #2 #3

⊙ Energy from Fossil Fuels

Fossil fuels come from animals and plants that died a very long time ago. The energy from those animals and plants is stored in the fossil fuel. Coal, oil, and natural gas are fossil fuels.

Fossil fuels are burned. Their stored energy is released. **Coal** is burned to make electricity. **Oil** is burned as gasoline. **Natural gas** is burned to heat houses.

After stored energy is burned, it cannot be used again.

Coal is used to make electricity ⊙
for homes and businesses.

⊙ Oil is used to make gasoline and
diesel fuel for cars, trucks, and farm
equipment.

Many houses have ⊙
stoves, clothes dryers,
and water heaters that
use natural gas. Natural
gas is also used to heat
homes. It can also be
used as fuel for some
cars, buses, and trucks.

Heat Energy

Heat is a kind of energy.

Heat always moves from where there is more heat to where there is less heat.

Heat moves in air and liquids. Hot air and liquids rise, or move up. Cold air and liquids fall, or move down. Hot smoke rises through the cooler air around it.

Heat moves between things that touch each other. When you take a bath in warm water, your body warms up. The warm water touches your cool body.

Heat moves through the air. You do not have to touch a fire to feel that it is hot.

GO ONLINE

To learn more about energy, check out these Web sites!

- **Be an Energy Star**
  http://www.energystar.gov/index.cfm?c=kids.kids_index
- **Energy Kids**
  http://tonto.eia.doe.gov/kids/
- **Chain Reaction Machine**
  http://pbskids.org/zoom/activities/sci/
  chainreactionmachine.html

Sound

What Is Sound?

Brrring! Class has begun. You know because you hear the bell ringing. Inside a bell, there is a piece of metal that moves back and forth. It bangs against the metal sides of the bell. This banging makes the bell vibrate (VY brayt). It makes the air vibrate, too. To **vibrate** means to move back and forth very quickly. These vibrations move through the air and into your ears. You sense them as sound!

Sound is a form of energy that is made when objects vibrate. These vibrations are called **sound waves**.

Like waves in water, sound waves can be big or little. They can travel for miles, or fade away in just a few feet. It all depends on how much energy they have.

◉ Sound vibrations are energy that moves through the air.

A tiny mosquito buzzes in your ear. What you hear is the vibrating of its wings. A train roars past you. You hear the vibrations of its wheels rolling on the tracks. You might even feel the train's sound energy moving through your body. A mosquito and a train create very different amounts of energy. Each travels through the air as sound.

⊙ A pencil moving on paper makes very little sound.

⊙ A plane makes a lot of sound.

See also:
page
220

Energy

CHECK YOUR ANSWERS
ON PAGES 314–329!

LISTEN UP!

Listen to the sounds all around you. Record what you hear in a chart.

1. Sit as quietly as possible and listen.
2. Make a chart like the one on this page to record each sound you can hear.
3. Mark how much energy you think each sound has.
4. Do you think a sound that comes from far away has more, less, or the same energy as a sound from nearby?

How Much Energy Do Sounds Have?

SOUNDS I CAN HEAR	 a LOT!	some.	VERY LiTTLe

Hearing Sound

Your ears help you hear sound. Your brain receives signals from the ears and tells you what you are hearing.

The curved shape of your ear is perfect for catching sound waves. Make a cone out of paper, and hold it to your ear. Listen to how this shape makes hearing easier.

Your eardrums are sensitive. Rub your thumb and pointer finger together next to your ear. You can clearly hear the sound even though the vibrations moving through the air are tiny.

Loud sounds are much easier to hear. But very loud sounds can hurt your eardrum.

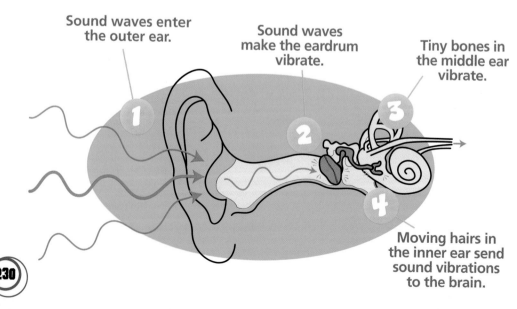

Sound waves enter the outer ear.

Sound waves make the eardrum vibrate.

Tiny bones in the middle ear vibrate.

Moving hairs in the inner ear send sound vibrations to the brain.

Volume

A sound can be soft or loud. It depends on how big the vibrations are. Something with more energy and force makes bigger vibrations. It will be loud. Something with less energy and force makes smaller vibrations. It will be quiet. **Volume** is how loud or quiet a sound is.

This caterpillar's legs create a tiny force as they move across the leaf, so they make tiny sound waves as well.

Sound vibrations move like waves through matter. Drop a tiny pebble into water. Small waves will drift away from the spot where the pebble hit. Now drop a huge rock. The waves will be much bigger and travel much farther. Sound waves work in a similar way.

A building being torn down creates a huge amount of energy and force, so it creates huge sound waves.

GLAD SCIENTIST

check your answers, pages 314-329

LET'S HEAR IT FOR SOUND!

Make loud and soft sounds to explore the energy in sound waves.

1. Clap as quietly as you can but so that you can still hear a sound. What do you feel in your hands?
2. Now clap as loudly as possible. What do you feel in your hands this time?
3. Why does clapping loudly feel different from clapping softly? What does this tell you about sound?

Pitch

Sounds can also be high or low. This is called **pitch**. The chirping of a bird is a high-pitched sound. The mooing of a cow is a low-pitched sound. Listen to the sounds around you. They all have pitch.

Pitch depends on the speed of the vibrations. A small bell makes a high-pitched sound. The sound vibrations are moving quickly. A large bell makes a low-pitched sound. It has slow vibrations.

Woof! Woof! A big ◉ dog's bark vibrates the air slowly, so it is a low-pitched sound.

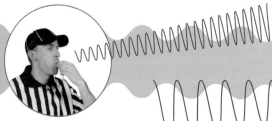

◉ Tweeeet! This whistle vibrates quickly when it is blown, so it produces a high-pitched sound.

Is It High or Low?

Name something with a high-pitched sound and a low-pitched sound. Write your answers in your science notebook.

find answers on 314 – 329

When you speak, air moves through special folds inside your throat called the **vocal cords**. The vocal cords vibrate and make sound when air goes over them. The sides of the vocal cords can get longer or shorter. This is how you can make low-pitched sounds or high-pitched sounds.

◉ When you open your mouth wide and say "ahhh" for the doctor, you can feel your vocal cords vibrate.

GLaD SCieNTiST

CHeCK YouR aNSweRS, PaGeS 314-329

MuSiCaL GLasSeS

See how water in a glass affects the pitch of sound.

1. Find five glasses. They should be the same size and shape.
2. Pour different amounts of water in four glasses. Leave one glass empty.
3. Use a pencil to lightly tap each glass. How does the amount of water in each glass change its pitch?
4. Why do you think the pitch changes?

How Sound Travels

Most of the sounds that we hear travel through air. If you are underwater though, you will still hear sounds. In fact, sound travels faster and farther through solids and liquids than it does through air.

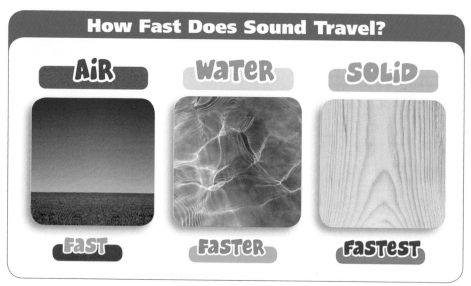

How Fast Does Sound Travel?

AiR	WATER	SOLiD
Fast	Faster	Fastest

Is That a Fact?

A Whale of a Song

Deep in the ocean, a humpback whale sings. His call goes out through miles of water. No one knows for sure why he sings. Scientists do know that these songs can travel very far through the ocean. Sound travels faster through water than through air. Very far away, another whale hears the song. He begins to sing back.

When sound waves hit a solid surface, they will bounce back to you as an **echo**. It will take the echo a few seconds to come back if the surface is far away. You will hear an echo of what you just said. If you are too close to the surface, you will not hear the echo. It will return before you have even finished speaking!

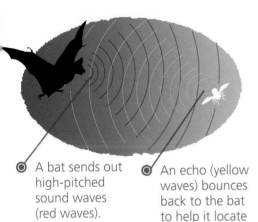

Some bats use echoes to help them find food, such as insects, in the dark. As a bat flies, it will make a very loud, high-pitched sound from its mouth or nose. It is so high pitched that humans cannot hear this sound. The sound travels through the air until it hits an insect. The sound

A bat sends out high-pitched sound waves (red waves).

An echo (yellow waves) bounces back to the bat to help it locate the insect.

waves bounce back to the bat as an echo. The bat uses the echo to find the insect. The bat's ability to do this is called **echolocation** (ek oh loh KAY shuhn). Echolocation is also used by whales to talk to each other.

GO ONLINE

To learn more about sound, check out these Web sites!

- **Visit an online sound library**
  http://www.pdsounds.org/
- **Listen to whale songs**
  http://lawrencehallofscience.org/whale/
- **Make your own instruments**
  http://mudcat.org/kids/

Musical Sounds

Musical instruments have parts that vibrate. Each instrument has its own special way of making music.

Guitar The strings of a guitar are all the same length. When you pluck the strings, they vibrate. You press the strings against the guitar's neck to change their pitch. A thick string vibrates slowly and makes a lower sound. A thin string vibrates quickly and makes a higher sound.

Piano A piano makes a sound when you hit the keys. Each key is attached to a hammer inside the piano. The hammer strikes a string, which causes the string to vibrate. Shorter and tighter strings have a high-pitched sound. Longer and looser strings have a low-pitched sound. A special board in the piano helps to make the sound louder.

Pressing on a piano key (left) causes a hammer to strike a string (right), making a sound.

236

Saxophone When you blow into a saxophone, the reed—a small flat piece of wood—vibrates. These vibrations move through the tubes of the sax. The sax also has valves that can cover holes in the tube. The more holes that are covered, the lower the sound. The fewer holes covered, the higher the sound.

Trumpet You have to vibrate your lips when you blow through a trumpet. The vibrations move through a long tube. When you press down on a valve, you block off part of the tube. The length of the tube is what makes higher or lower notes. A long tube of air vibrates slowly and makes low-pitched sounds. A shorter tube of air vibrates quickly, which makes the sound higher.

History *Makers*

Thomas Alva Edison (1847–1931)

Thomas Edison showed the world how to record sound. He used sound vibrations to make marks in a piece of tinfoil. When a needle was dragged across the marks, it vibrated, too. The needle's vibrations made a sound that was just like the sound Edison had begun with!

237

Light

What Is Light?

See also:
page
228
Sound

Flip a switch, and a room fills with light. It fills with energy, too. **Light** is energy that moves in waves. Light can come from a lamp, a fire, or the Sun. Light always moves through space in straight lines called **rays**.

See also:
page
168
The Solar System

Light waves move in straight lines as they leave a source of light.

● You can see the Sun's rays shining in straight lines through the trees.

Light waves move through matter. Light waves can move through empty space, too.

● The energy of sunlight travels through millions of miles of empty space to reach Earth.

Is That a Fact

Fast as Lightning

Sound waves move quickly, but light travels even faster: about 300,000 kilometers (186,000 miles) per *second*! That is why you can see lightning before you can hear thunder.

Light is also why we can see. Light enters the eye through the cornea. Cells at the back of the eye change the light into messages. These messages are sent to the brain. In a split second, the brain knows what we are seeing!

DiaGRam OF THe EYe

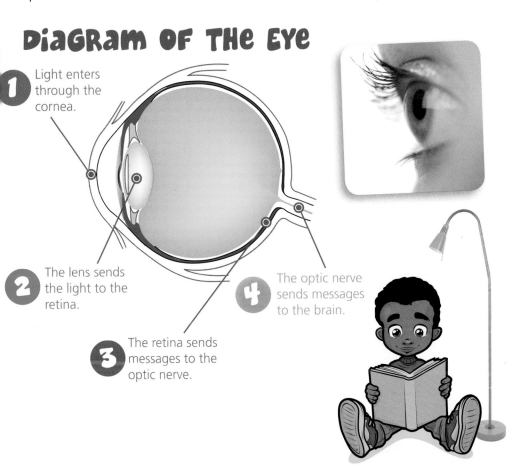

1 Light enters through the cornea.

2 The lens sends the light to the retina.

3 The retina sends messages to the optic nerve.

4 The optic nerve sends messages to the brain.

where-Do-we-Get-Light?

Name as many things as you can think of that give us light. Write your answers in your science notebook.

FIND ANSWERS on 314 - 329

◉ Light and Heat

The Sun is Earth's best source of light and heat. Plants take in energy from sunlight to make the energy they need to grow. If plants do not grow, animals—including humans—cannot eat.

Without sunlight, ◉ we would not be able to grow food.

Sunlight also brings **heat energy** to Earth. Without heat, all the water on our planet would be ice. Earth would be much too cold to support life.

◉ Sunlight brings heat and light to Earth.

You can feel the Sun's **light energy** on your skin on a warm day.

Wearing sunscreen ◉ protects your skin from the strong rays of the Sun.

Things that give off light often give off heat. The energy in sunlight is what keeps Earth warm. Hold your hand near a light bulb, and you can feel just how much heat energy it has.

See also:
page
220
Energy

◉ A campfire gives off light, but it gives off a lot of heat, too. That's good news when you want to roast marshmallows!

The energy in sunlight can ◉ make a sidewalk hot enough to fry an egg—or burn your feet!

See also:
page
168
The Solar System

◉ The Sun's rays pass through the glass roof of a greenhouse. These light waves heat up the inside of the greenhouse, which helps the plants to grow.

The link between light and heat works the other way, too. If you make a piece of metal hot enough, it will begin to glow. Heat and light often work together.

When a stove burner ◉ becomes very hot, it gives off light waves.

Reflection

Light waves travel in a straight line until they reach an object.

Some light waves bounce off an object and back to our eyes. This is called **reflection** (ri FLEK shuhn). We see objects because of reflected light. Most things reflect some light. The Moon reflects light from the Sun.

If an object is very shiny and smooth, the light waves reflect in a special way. They hit the surface and then bounce back in the exact same pattern. Hold a mirror up in front of you. You'll see that all the light waves from the room—and your face—will bounce back.

◉ If you look straight into a mirror, you can see your reflection.

You can see a reflection of the ◉ landscape in a smooth lake.

Is That a Fact?

Mirror, Mirror on the Wall

Mirrors aren't just polished glass. Behind the glass is a thin coating of metal. Metal reflects light waves much better than glass does. You see your reflection through the glass, but it's the metal that's doing the reflecting.

The Passage of Light

Transparent objects let most light pass through them. Clear glass and air are transparent. You can see through transparent objects.

Transparent
Most light passes through

Translucent objects let some light pass through them. The rest of the light scatters. You can see through translucent objects, but not as well. Tissue paper and lamp shades are translucent.

Translucent
Some light passes through

Opaque objects do not let light pass through them. Most things are opaque. Desks and books are opaque. You are opaque. You cannot see through opaque objects.

Opaque
No light passes through

GLAD SCIENTIST

CHECK YOUR ANSWERS, PAGES 314-329!

LIGHT COMING THROUGH!

See how much light travels through different materials.

1. Make a chart with three columns. Label the columns "Opaque," "Translucent," and "Transparent."
2. Try to find different kinds of objects. They can be made of paper, wool, plastic, or cotton.
3. Hold each object up in front of a bright light. How much light passes through it? Record what you see in the chart.

Refraction

Light waves bend when they move from one kind of matter into another. This is called **refraction** (ri FRAK shuhn).

Place a straight straw into a clear glass of water. The straw looks bent! Why? It is not the straw that is bending. It is the light. The light bends when it moves from the air into the water.

◉ Because of refraction, this straw looks like it is in two parts.

History *Makers*

Ibn al-Haytham (965–1040)

One thousand years ago, the Arab scholar al-Haytham wrote the *Book of Optics*. It was one of the first times refraction and color were explained.

GLAD SCIENTIST

CHECK YOUR ANSWERS, PAGES 314–329!

REFRACTION MAGIC

Use refraction to make a coin appear to float.

1. Place a coin inside a shallow bowl.
2. Walk backward. Stop when the rim of the bowl is just high enough block the coin from your view.
3. Have a friend pour water slowly into the bowl. Make sure the coin does not move.
4. As the water rises, the coin should reappear above the rim of the bowl. Do you know why you can see the coin again?

Shadows

Remember that light travels in a straight path. An opaque object that blocks the light makes a **shadow**.

◉ These children's bodies are blocking light waves and making shadows on the sand.

Point a bright light at a wall, and then dance in front of it. Your shadow will dance on the wall right along with you. When you dance in front of the light, your body blocks the light waves.

A shadow can have the shape of the object that makes it.

◉ You can make shadow puppets on the wall by shining a light behind your hands.

You can see the shadow ◉ of the bike and the person riding it.

Did **You** Know?

Sundials have been used for thousands of years to tell time. The Sun hits the pointer on the sundial. This causes a shadow to fall on a number, which tells the hour. This shadow moves throughout the day as the Sun appears to move across the sky.

245

Absorption

Light that isn't reflected is absorbed. **Absorption** (uhb SORP shuhn) means that the object takes in the light.

When light waves reach a clear substance, like glass or water, they move right through it. Most surfaces are opaque, though. When light meets opaque objects, some of the light is absorbed and some of it bounces away. The light that bounces away is reflected.

Look at the basketball. The ball reflects only orange light, so you see the ball as orange. The rest of the colors are absorbed.

Absorption and Reflection

COLOR

This object looks blue because it reflects only blue light.

White

This object reflects all light, so it looks white.

Black

This object absorbs all the light, so it looks black.

GO ONLINE

To learn more about light, check out this Web site!

- **Watch a color wheel spin**
  http://pbskids.org/dragonflytv/superdoit/
  color_round_up.html

Color

Have you ever seen a rainbow after it rains? Light from the Sun bends as it passes through the raindrops. The light breaks up into colors. This is called the **color spectrum**. The colors in the color spectrum are red, orange, yellow, green, blue, indigo, and violet.

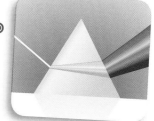

A prism divides light into its separate colors.

A rainbow is made when little drops of water in the air act like prisms.

CHECK YOUR ANSWERS ON PAGES 314–329!

GET THE MESSAGE

make the connection Use the properties of light to read a secret message.

1. Use a blue marker to write a secret message on a white sheet of paper.

2. Use yellow, red, and green markers to scribble designs on top of your message. Be sure that the original message cannot be read.

3. Trade sheets with another student. Using red, yellow, green, and blue cellophane, try to read the message. Can you do it? If so, explain how. Why does the cellophane help you read the message?

Motion and Forces

What Is Motion?

If you put a pencil on your desk, it will not move unless you pick it up. **Motion** is when something moves from one place to another.

There are almost as many ways to move as there are things that move. A hot air balloon moves up, and a parachute moves down. You might run to the left or hop to the right. A sprinter runs forward to reach the finish line. A softball player runs backward to make a catch.

Everywhere you look, something moves. The world is in motion.

SOME TYPES OF MOTION

Curved

Zigzag

Straight

Circular

Up

Down

Sometimes motion is so slow you hardly notice it. An hour hand moving around a clock is very slow. Other times, motion is very fast. Think how fast a shooting star flashes across the night sky. **Speed** is how fast or slow something moves.

Cars on a road are faster than bikes. A plane is faster than a train. Things move at different speeds.

An ostrich cannot fly, but it can run very fast.

Sloths get around by crawling very slowly.

CHECK YOUR ANSWERS ON PAGES 314–329!

make THE connection

On the Move!

Explore the different ways things move in the world around you.

1. Make a list in your science notebook of different kinds of motion.

2. Walk around your school or neighborhood. Look for moving things. How did they move? Write each one down on your list.

3. Which things moved in different ways?

4. Did everything move at the same speed?

What Is Force?

Everything moves because of force. **Force** causes objects to start moving or stop moving. You use force when you push or pull an object.

Force can even cause objects to change direction. Blow a soap bubble, and it will move straight out from the wand. Your breath was the force that pushed it. Right away, though, the wind will push the bubble in another direction. The wind has a force that changed the bubble's path.

Pull · or · Push

Which pictures show a pulling force, and which ones show a pushing force?

FIND ANSWERS ON 314 - 329

When you kick a ball, the force of your foot is what makes it move. A hammer hitting a nail has enough force to push the nail into wood.

See also:
page
256
Magnetism

When you ride a bike, you apply force to the pedals. That force is what gets you to move. If you want to move at a higher speed, then you pedal with more force.

See also:
page
264
Simple Machines

 ◉ A paddle pushing against water is a force that moves the boat.

 ◉ A tennis player uses a lot of force when he serves.

A magnet has a ◉ force that pulls some metals.

When you walk, ◉ your foot pushes down and the ground pushes up with the same force.

GLAD SCIENTIST
CHECK YOUR ANSWERS,
Pages 314-329!

WHaT'S THE WORD?

Make a chart like the one below. List some things in motion. Then use the lines to tell about their motion. The first answer has been done for you as an example.

	Type of Motion	Speed	Amount of Force
1. snail	straight	very slow	very little
2. train			
3. falling snow			
4. swing			

Gravity

Watch a boulder roll down a hill. Drop a pencil, and it will fall to the ground. Jump as high as you can, but you will always return to Earth. Everything that goes up must come down.

All objects pull on each other with a special force. This special force is called **gravity**. All objects have gravity. It is the force that pulls objects toward each other. Earth has the most gravity because it is the biggest thing around! When you drop something, it falls to the ground unless something stops it. Why? Because gravity pulls it toward Earth.

Gravity is pulling this ball down to the ground, but the boy's hand stops it.

Gravity pulls a snowboarder down a hill.

Force of Gravity

Force of Chair

Gravity keeps us sitting in our chairs.

Jump, and gravity brings you back to Earth.

Gravity can be very weak or very powerful. It depends on two things. One thing is distance. Objects that are far away from each other have less gravity than objects that are close. The other thing is mass. **Mass** is a measure of how much matter there is in an object. An object with a lot of mass is heavy, such as a bowling ball. An object with little mass is light, such as a feather.

See also: page **168** The Solar System

Earth has more mass than the Moon. ◉ Earth's gravity pulls on the Moon so that it does not float away into space.

See also: page **212** Matter

make the connection — Hang On!

CHECK YOUR ANSWERS ON PAGES 314–329!

Use a milk carton, marbles, a paper clip, and a rubber band to explore the force of gravity.

Remember! Safety first! Wear goggles.

1. Make a chart like this one.

2. Poke a paper clip into the carton. Attach a rubber band to the paper clip. Hold the rubber band, and hang the milk carton a few feet above ground.

3. Add ten marbles to the carton. Measure the length of the rubber band. Record this number in the chart.

4. Add five marbles at a time. Measure the length of the rubber band each time. What force causes the rubber band to stretch?

MILK

Marbles	Length
5	
10	
15	
20	
25	
30	
35	
40	
45	
50	

Friction

Two things rubbing together causes friction. **Friction** is a force that makes moving objects slow down or stop. The smooth, plastic surface of a slide lets you zoom to the ground. There is little friction when your clothing rubs against the slide. If the surface was rough concrete, you might not slide at all. Rough surfaces create more friction.

◎ The brakes on a bike use friction to help you stop the bike.

There is little ◎
friction on a slide.

Weight also makes more friction. Pushing one book across the floor is pretty easy. Pushing a whole bookcase across the floor is much harder. There is a lot more friction.

◎ Friction creates heat. Rub your hands together, and you can feel them get warmer.

Is That a Fact

Slip and Sled

Friction helps a sled slide better. When a sled zips downhill, there is friction between the runners and the snow. This friction creates heat, which melts the snow. Soon, the sled is gliding along on a thin layer of water!

Buoyancy

Throw a rock into water, and it sinks. Gravity pulls it down into the water. Then put a raft into the water. Even though the raft is larger than the rock, it floats. A force in the water called **buoyancy** (BOY uhn see) pushes up on the raft. Buoyancy keeps the raft from sinking.

◎ A rock has less surface area than a raft does, so it sinks.

In order to float, an object has to have enough surface area to push the water out of the way. Water that is pushed out of the way has a lot of force. The force of the water makes the object float.

The shape of an object can make it sink or float, too. A lump of clay sinks to the bottom. But shape the clay into a boat. Then it will float!

A raft is large, but it ◎ can float on water.

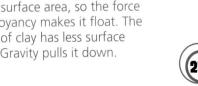

Gravity

Buoyancy

◎ The boat made of clay has more surface area, so the force of buoyancy makes it float. The lump of clay has less surface area. Gravity pulls it down.

(255)

Magnetism

What Is Magnetism?

Magnetism (MAG nuh ti zuhm) is a force. A **force** is any push or pull. Magnets can pull things without touching them. Objects that have this force are called magnets. **Magnets** cannot move everything, though. Magnetism works on things that are made only of iron or a few other kinds of metal.

See also:
page
248
Motion and Forces

Magnets can be shaped like bars or donuts. Sometimes they are shaped like horseshoes. Whatever a magnet's shape is, it has a force that can work at a distance.

GLaD SCieNTiST
CHeCK YOUR aNsWeRS, PaGes 314-329

A MaGNeTiC iNVeSTiGaTioN

Find out which objects are attracted to a magnet. Make a chart to record your results.

1. Gather 10 objects from around the room. Be sure at least half of them contain some metal.
2. Predict which objects will be pulled by the magnet.
3. Test each object by putting the magnet near it. Record your finding
4. Look at your results. Are they what you predicted? Did any result surprise you? If the magnet pulled an object, what does that tell you

Magnets can pull, but they can push, too. When the ends of two magnets are brought together, they can push each other away.

Each end of a magnet is called a pole. Every magnet has two poles—the **north pole** (N) and the **south pole** (S). If you point the N pole of one magnet at the S pole of another magnet, they will pull together. Opposites attract.

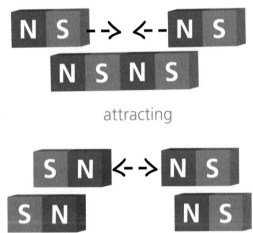

attracting

If you point the same poles at each other, the magnets will push apart. Two N poles or two S poles will repel each other.

repelling

CHECK YOUR ANSWERS
ON PAGES 314-329!

WHICH END IS WHICH?

Explore the pushing and pulling forces between two magnets.

1. Wrap a bar magnet and a horseshoe magnet in masking tape. Make sure you can't see any marks telling which poles are which.

2. Push one end of the bar magnet toward the right side of the horseshoe magnet. Do the magnets attract or repel each other?

3. If they attract each other, draw a circle on that end of the bar magnet. Draw an X on the right side of the horseshoe magnet. If they repel each other, mark an X in both places.

4. Predict what will happen when you push the unmarked ends of the magnets together. Then try it. Did you predict correctly? Explain your answer.

Magnetic Fields

A magnet is surrounded by a magnetic field. You cannot see it, but this field is where the magnetic force is found. The force is always strongest at the poles. The sides of a magnet still have force, but it is weaker.

A **magnetic field** is strongest close to a magnet. It is weaker where the field is farther away from the magnet. Push a magnet slowly toward a paper clip. When the clip just begins to move, you've found the edge of the magnetic field. Keep pushing and the paper clip will move toward the magnet and stick to it. That is where the magnetic force is at its strongest.

◉ The magnetic field around a magnet depends on the shape of the magnet.

◉ The magnetic force reaches out into the space around a magnet. This picture shows the shape of the magnetic fields around the two bar magnets.

Is That a Fact?

Pole Power

If you cut a magnet in half, the two halves will not have just one pole each. Both of the new pieces will still have N and S poles. You can cut a magnet into smaller and smaller pieces, but every time, each piece will have both poles.

Most refrigerators have at least a couple of magnets on them. Some refrigerators are covered with them. The magnets might hold pictures or lists. Some pens or clocks even have magnets so that they can be stuck to the refrigerator.

A magnetic field that holds a picture on the fridge moves through matter. It goes through paper and paint to reach the metal of the refrigerator. Magnetic fields can move through most kinds of matter.

GLaD ScientisT

CHECK YOUR ANSWERS, PAGES 314-329!

MagneTism coming Through!

Explore the properties of magnetic fields.

1. Find different containers. Look for ones that are made of glass, plastic, and metal. They should have different shapes, too. Find ones that are wide, narrow, and in-between.
2. Fill the containers with water. Drop a paper clip into each one.
3. Hold a magnet up to the outside of one of the containers. Does the paper clip move? What does this tell you about the magnetic field? Now, hold the magnet up to each of the other containers.
4. Did the paper clip move every time? If not, why?

Magnetic Earth

Each magnet has an N pole and an S pole. As you know, Earth has North and South Poles. The N pole of a magnet gets its name because it is attracted to Earth's **North Pole**. The S pole of a magnet is attracted to Earth's **South Pole**. Magnets are attracted to Earth's poles because our planet is a magnet, too.

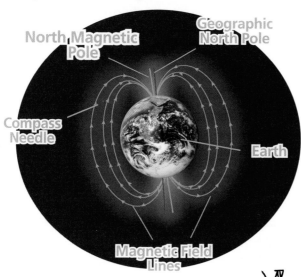

North Magnetic Pole

Geographic North Pole

Compass Needle

Earth

Magnetic Field Lines

◉ Earth's magnetic poles are where its magnetism is strongest. The North and South Poles are the ends of Earth's axis, which is the imaginary pole around which Earth spins.

Did You Know?

Dancing Lights of the North
The Northern Lights are a wonderful sight. Streaks of color move through the night sky.
What causes this amazing light show? It begins with tiny particles of matter from space. They are pushed through space by the Sun's energy. As they move past Earth, some of them enter Earth's magnetic field. They zip past other particles there. The movement makes electricity. It also gives off light. We see what looks like sheets of colored light dancing across the sky.

Compass

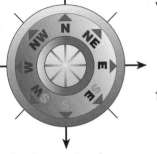

A **compass** is a special tool that uses magnetism. The needle inside a compass is a magnet. It is very light. It is attached to a post so that it can spin freely inside the case. No matter which way you face, the needle will turn so that it is pointing toward Earth's magnetic North Pole.

◉ The needle of a compass always points toward Earth's magnetic North Pole.

The point of the needle is its N pole. If you face north, the needle will point away from you. Turn to the left, and the needle will appear to turn to the right. It did not really move, though. It is still pointing to the north.

Remember! Be careful—needles are sharp!

GLaD SCieNTiST
Check your answers, pages 314–329.

MaKe YOUR POiNT!

Build your own working compass. You will need a needle, a cork, a magnet, and a shallow dish of water.

1. Rub the needle across the magnet 50 times. Always rub the needle in the same direction.
2. Have an adult cut a small, round piece off the cork. Ask the adult to push the needle through the circle of cork the long way, not through the center.
3. Float the cork and needle in the dish. Which way does the needle point? If you turn the dish, does the needle turn with it? Why do you think this happened?

Magnets and Technology

You learned how magnets are used in compasses. Here are some other ways magnets are put to use.

There is a giant magnet at the end of this crane. It is used to lift large metal scraps. Sometimes these magnets lift entire cars. The metal is dropped into a machine that crushes it into blocks. These blocks of metal are then ready to be recycled.

This is a maglev train. The word maglev is a short way of saying "magnetic levitation." These trains float above their tracks. There are magnets under the train, and there are magnets in the track. The magnets point the same poles at each other, which makes a pushing force. Remember, poles that are alike repel each other. The pushing force lifts the entire train off the track. Since the train is floating in the air, there is no friction. These trains can move very fast.

GO ONLINE

To learn more about making magnets, check out this Web site!

• **Funny Family Fridge Magnets**
  http://pbskids.org/zoom/activities/do/
  funnyfamilyfridgemag.html

Magnets Making Magnets
When you made a compass, the first step was rubbing the needle on a magnet. The needle became a magnet, too.

History **Makers**

Michael Faraday
(1791–1867)

Michael Faraday was a British scientist. In 1831, he made a discovery that changed the world. Faraday moved a magnet back and forth through a coil of wire. He saw that doing this made electricity flow through the wire. Faraday had shown the world that magnets and electricity are linked. What force was used to make electricity? Yes, it was magnetism.

SCIENCE NOTEBOOK

MATCH PLAY

Match each word with its definition. Write your answers in your science notebook.

1. Magnetic field
2. N Pole
3. S Pole
4. Magnet

a. will pull when put near an N pole
b. an object that can pull from a distance
c. strongest right next to a magnet
d. will push when put near an N pole

Simple Machines

What Is a Simple Machine?

Let's say you need to move 50 books from one shelf to another. Would you move all 50 books at once? Of course not. They would be too heavy to lift! Instead, you would make several trips from shelf to shelf. You would carry a few books at a time. You would still do the same amount of work. But you would not need to use as much force.

A **simple machine** uses the same idea. It makes work easier. When you use a simple machine, you use less force to do the job.

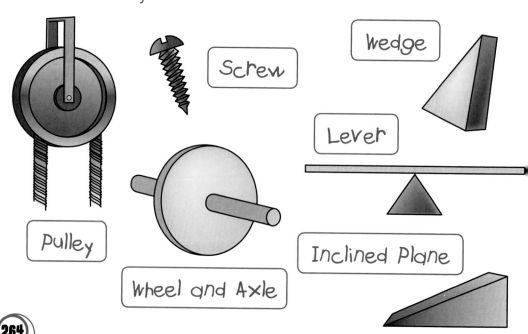

Screw

Wedge

Lever

Pulley

Wheel and Axle

Inclined Plane

Simple machines have been around for thousands of years. Can you find which pictures show a lever, a pulley, a wedge, and a wheel and axle?

CHECK YOUR ANSWERS
ON PAGES 314-329!

FIND THE MACHINE

make THE connection

Find simple machines you use every day.

1. Look around your classroom or playground.

2. Make a chart with six columns. Label the columns "Wheel and Axle," "Lever," "Inclined Plane," "Pulley," "Wedge," and "Screw."

3. See how many of each simple machine you can add to each column.

4. How do you use each of these simple machines?

⊙ Lever

A **lever** is a long bar or board. The bar turns on a point called the **fulcrum** (FUL kruhm). The fulcrum does not move. A lever can help you lift or move heavy objects.

A **force** is a push or a pull. If you use force at one end of the bar, you can make the bar turn on the fulcrum. The other end of the bar then moves in the opposite direction. If the fulcrum is close to the object you want to lift, then you can use less force.

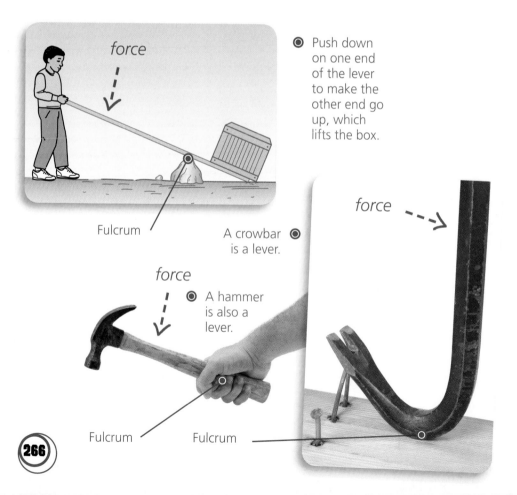

force

⊙ Push down on one end of the lever to make the other end go up, which lifts the box.

Fulcrum

A crowbar ⊙ is a lever.

force

⊙ A hammer is also a lever.

force

Fulcrum

Fulcrum

A balance scale is a lever in action. The bar stays level when you put the same amount of weight on both sides. Imagine putting something heavier on one side. Then gravity will pull on that side with more force. The bar will dip, and the side with more weight will sink lower.

See also: page **248**

Motion and Forces

A seesaw works like a balance scale.

Fulcrum

GLaD cientist

CHeck your answers, pages 314-329!

can i GeT a LiFT?

Explore how levers work by placing the fulcrum in different places.

1. Set up a simple lever using a long, flat board and a triangle-shaped block.
2. Place a brick or other heavy object at one end of the lever. Slide the fulcrum so that it is near the other end of the lever. Push down on the end of the bar closest to the fulcrum. Can you lift the object?
3. Slide the fulcrum to the center of the bar. Try to lift the object again. Can you lift the brick this time?
4. Slide the fulcrum so that it is near the brick. Lift the object one more time with the lever. Can you lift the brick? Where was the fulcrum when the brick was easiest to lift?

Wheel and Axle

A **wheel and axle** has two parts. The axle is a small rod that goes through the center of the wheel. When the axle turns, so does the wheel. The amount of force you use to turn the small axle also turns the much larger wheel. You can move an object from one place to another with a wheel and axle.

You can see the wheel and axle on an old car.

Wheel

Axle

A boat is steered using a wheel and axle.

A doorknob is a wheel. It is connected to an axle on the inside of the door.

The wheels and axles on a shopping cart make it easier to move things.

A screwdriver is also a wheel and axle.

Pulley

A **pulley** is made of rope and a wheel. The rope fits into a groove on the wheel. When force is applied to the rope, the wheel spins. A pulley is used to lift an object up, down, or sideways.

For instance, a pulley makes it easy to lift a heavy object. You can do this by attaching an object to one end of the rope. When you pull down on the other end of the rope, you can lift the object.

A crane uses ⊚ pulleys to lift heavy loads.

⊚ These pulleys are used on a sailboat. You can see that the groove in the wheels holds the ropes in place.

This pulley ⊚ can lift a bucket of water from a well.

⊚ A clothesline uses a pulley to move clothes back and forth.

Inclined Plane

An **inclined plane** is about as simple as a machine can be. It is a tilted surface. A ramp is an inclined plane. Pushing something heavy up a ramp takes less force than lifting it straight up.

Ladders are also inclined planes. They help people move up or down.

Stairs are a form of an inclined plane that you use often. You could never jump high enough to reach the second floor of a building. A single step up is easy, though. Take a dozen or so steps, and you will have gone up one flight of stairs.

A ramp makes it easy for a person in a wheelchair to go up or down.

◉ You can easily walk up an inclined plane.

Is That a Fact?

Stacking King-Sized Blocks

The stone blocks used to build the Great Pyramid were very heavy. There was no electricity in ancient Egypt. But there were inclined planes. Historians think the heavy blocks were dragged and pushed up ramps!

Wedge

A **wedge** is used to split things. Anything with a sharp edge or a pointed end can be used as a wedge. Knives, nails, axes, and needles are all examples of wedges.

If you want to split a log into two pieces, you could try to rip it in half. But it would take a huge amount of force to do it. An axe lets you split the log with much less force. As the axe moves through the log, its wedge shape pushes the sides apart. The axe does a lot of the work for you.

The pointed end of a nail is also a wedge. It helps split the wood as a nail is pounded into a board.

An axe has a wedge.

◉ A wedge can split a log.

◉ A wedge allows a plow to cut through grass and soil.

◉ The wedge on a nail makes it easier to drive into wood.

Screw

A **screw** is a long inclined plane wrapped around a rod. A screw is used to hold things together. Like the wedge at the end of a nail, a screw's inclined plane helps it split wood.

The threads of a  screw are really one long inclined plane.

A screw uses less force to split wood than a nail does.

A propeller works like a screw.  As a screw turns, it pulls itself into the wood. As a propeller turns, it pulls itself—and the plane—through the air.

Which-Is-Which?

For each job described below, choose the simple machine that would be the most help. Write your answers in your science notebook.

PULLEY   LEVER   WEDGE

1. You want to pull old nails out of a board.
2. You want to cut a limb off a tree.
3. You want to lift a huge sack of flour to the top of a high shelf.

FIND ANSWERS ON 514 - 529

Compound Machines

Simple machines can work together. A **compound machine** uses two or more simple machines. Compound machines are all around you.

For instance, a bicycle uses several simple machines. The hand brakes are levers. The chain and gears are a pulley. Screws attach parts to the bike. And the bike rolls along on two wheels and axles.

A bicycle is ◎ a compound machine.

Lever

Scissors are ◎ both a lever and a wedge.

Fulcrum

Wedges

Pulley

Wheel and Axle

◎ A can opener uses a wedge to split the lid from the can. The wedge is on a wheel that turns on an axle. The handles are levers.

Study Guide

Don't stop now—there is still a lot more to learn! Read about what scientists are working on these days. Learn how to read a map or to weigh your shoes. The science fun hasn't stopped yet!

Reading Maps

What Is a Map?

A **map** is a drawing that shows where things are located. Some maps show whole countries. Other maps show the rooms in a house. There are maps of zoos and parks. There are even maps of the Moon!

This map shows how to get to Washington, D.C.

Maps have many purposes. A map can tell you where something is and how to get there. It also can tell you how far one place is from another.

You can use a map to find the nearest library—or even to find buried treasure!

Use a world map to compare continents.

Types of Maps

There are many types of maps.

A **physical map** shows natural features like mountains and lakes. This map shows mountains in brown and lowlands in green.

Physical map

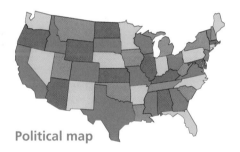

Political map

A **political map** shows the borders around areas such as states or countries.

A **thematic** (thee MAT ik) **map** shows information about a theme. This map shows the location of three types of grassland.

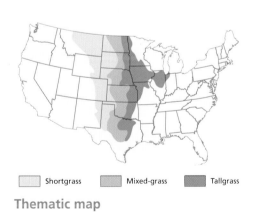

Shortgrass   Mixed-grass   Tallgrass

Thematic map

Parts of a Map

Maps must be easy to read. That's why most maps show only a certain amount of information. But there are some things you will find on every map.

1 A **map title** tells what the map is about.

2 A **map legend** tells what the symbols on the map stand for.

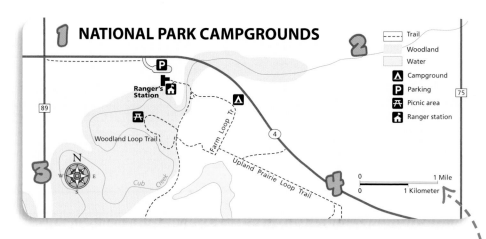

NATIONAL PARK CAMPGROUNDS

Trail
Woodland
Water
Campground
Parking
Picnic area
Ranger station

Ranger's Station

Woodland Loop Trail

Farm Loop Tr.

Upland Prairie Loop Trail

Cub Creek

89

75

4

0   1 Mile
0   1 Kilometer

3 A **compass rose** shows directions: north (N), south (S), east (E), and west (W).

4 A **map scale** compares a measurement on the map with the real distance in the world.

N

◉ North is usually at the top of a map. That means south is at the bottom, east is to the right, and west is to the left.

1 INCH on this map
equals
5 MILES at the campground

Some maps use a **grid** to help you find the exact location of something on the map. A grid has columns and rows that cross to form boxes. Each box is labeled with the letter and number of the column and the row that form it.

The blue triangle is at B3. The purple diamond is at D2.

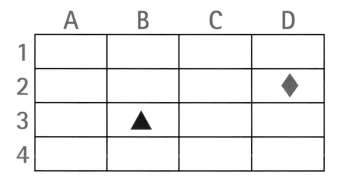

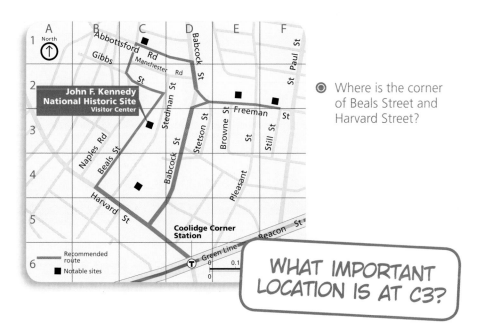

Where is the corner of Beals Street and Harvard Street?

WHAT IMPORTANT LOCATION IS AT C3?

How To Read a Map

You can learn to read a map just like a scientist does!

Look at the map below. This is a map of Rain's neighborhood. You can use this map to find

• the distance between places

• where places are located

• how to get from one place to another

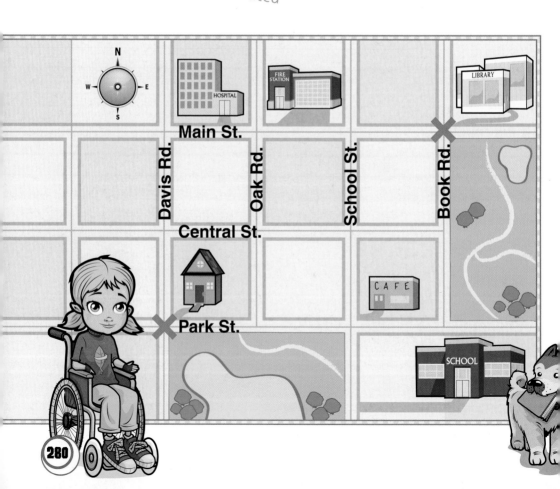

Rain and Rocket are going to the library!

Use the map to find out how they will get there.

1. Rain and Rocket live at the corner of Park Street and Davis Road.

2. The library is at Book Road and Main Street. That means the library is northeast of Rain's house.

3. Rain and Rocket must travel north and east from their house to reach the library.

> They can go east on Park Street to Book Road. Then they will go north on Book Road to the library.

> Or they can go north on Davis Road to Main Street. Then they will go east on Main Street to the library.

No matter which way they go, Rain and Rocket will travel north and east to reach the library.

Ask your teacher or your parents to help you draw a map of your neighborhood. Then use it to find different ways to get around!

How Scientists Use Maps

Scientists use many types of maps. They use thematic maps to get information and display data.

Oceanographers (oh shun AW gra fers) use maps that show features on the ocean floor.

Space scientists use maps to study space objects. This map of Mars tracks the path that the Mars Rover traveled!

Climatologists (kly muh TOL oh jists) use maps to show rainfall and temperatures.

Marine biologists use maps to track whale migrations.

HAWAII'S BIG ISLAND: ROAD MAP

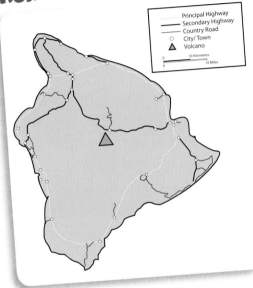

Principal Highway
Secondary Highway
Country Road
○ City/Town
▲ Volcano

Scientists also use maps just like we do: to find where something is located and how to get there.

These scientists used a road map to find the way to reach the top of this volcano.

Then they used a thematic map to find out which areas were safe and which were dangerous.

Visiting a Volcano

HAWAII'S BIG ISLAND: VOLCANO DANGER ZONES

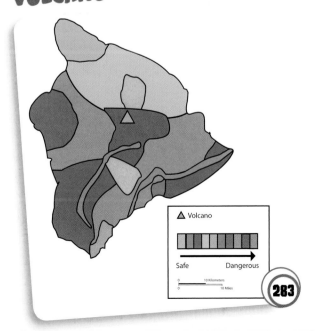

▲ Volcano

Safe   Dangerous

Science and Math Together

How Do Scientists Use Math?

A scientist measures things to get information.

There are two ways to measure things: the English system and the metric system. Each system uses different units.

Weight The English system measures weight in ounces and pounds. The metric system uses grams and kilograms.

Weight

English System	
1 pound =	16 ounces

Metric System	
1 kilogram =	1,000 grams

HOW Heavy?

6 ounces
(160 grams)

The Original Ounce

Ancient traders weighed goods in units based on grain!

1 GRAIN = the weight of 1 BARLEY SEED
and
438 GRAINS = about 1 OUNCE

Length

English System	
1 foot =	12 inches
1 yard =	3 feet
1 mile =	5,280 feet

Metric System	
1 meter =	100 centimeters
1 kilometer =	1,000 meters

Length The English system measures length by the inch, foot, yard, and mile.

The metric system uses the centimeter, meter, and kilometer.

HOW BiG aROUND?
9 inches
(23 centimeters)

HOW WiDE?
8 ½ inches
(22 centimeters)

HOW LONG?
11 inches
(28 centimenters)

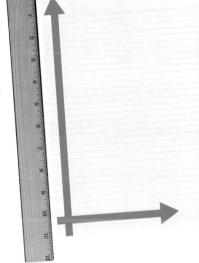

Whose Foot Is It Anyway?

The ancient world based the length of
A FOOT
on the length of
THE KING'S FOOT!

Volume The English system of measurements is used in the United States for cooking. It is also used for measuring products you buy in the store. For example, you can buy 6 ounces of shampoo or one pound of nails. The milliliter and the liter are metric units of volume.

Volume

English System	
1 tablespoon =	3 teaspoons
1 fluid ounce =	2 tablespoons
1 pint =	16 fluid ounces
1 quart =	32 fluid ounces
1 gallon =	64 fluid ounces
Metric System	
1 liter =	1,000 milliliters

1 liter

1 quart

WHiCH OUNCE iS WHiCH?

The English system has two types of ounces.

The **fluid ounce** measures volume. That's how much space something takes up.

A **dry ounce** measures weight. That's how heavy something is.

Temperature You can measure temperature in two ways.

The Fahrenheit scale measures temperature in degrees Fahrenheit (°F).

In the Celsius scale, temperature is measured in degrees Celsius (°C).

Temperature

Fahrenheit scale
Water freezes at 32°F
Water boils at 212°F

Celsius scale
Water freezes at 0°C
Water boils at 100°C

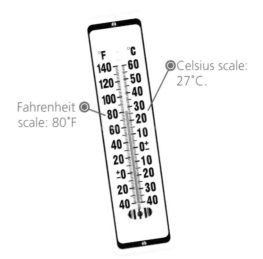

Fahrenheit scale: 80°F

Celsius scale: 27°C.

BEACH TIME:
above 85°F
(around 30°C)

SWEATER WEATHER:
below 45°F
(below 7°C)

Cool Scientists

Life Science

Life scientists study living things and their environment.

Galapagos tortoise

When Carole Baldwin goes to work, she goes swimming! Dr. Baldwin is a marine biologist. That's a scientist who studies ocean organisms. She also starred in the Smithsonian 3-D IMAX film, *Galapagos*.

Marine biologists study biology. They also know a lot about oceans and climate.

Do you like museums? Petra Sierwald does! She's a museum curator at Chicago's Field Museum. A curator uses art and science. The art part? Designing exhibits! The science part? For Dr. Sierwald, that's studying spiders and millipedes.

Redkne
tarantu

Tree frog

African savannah

Jobs in Life Science

Conservation Biologist
(endangered species)

Primatologist
(apes and monkeys)

Fingerprint Technician
(crime scene investigation)

Veterinarian
(animal doctor)

Earth Science

Some Earth scientists study Earth's physical features and processes. Some study weather. And some study the universe!

Doug Ming

Doug Ming is a planetary scientist with NASA. He wants to grow plants on the Moon and Mars! For now, he studies how plants grow in different types of environments—like Antarctica!

Planetary scientists must know about geology and astronomy. They also use math and physics.

Paul Sereno is a paleontologist. He hunts fossils all over the world! He discovered fossils of the first dinosaurs to roam Earth: *Herrerasaurus* and *Eoraptor*! Paleontologists usually study geology and biology.

Dinosaur Fossil

Jobs in Earth Science

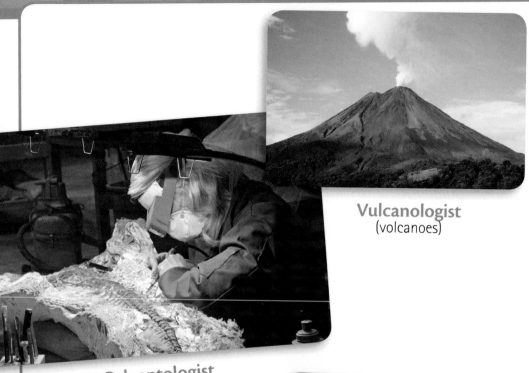

Vulcanologist
(volcanoes)

Paleontologist
(fossils)

Astronomer
(stars and planets)

Soil Scientist
(soil)

Physical Science

Dr. Duilia De Mello

From atoms to galaxies, scientists use physical science to understand the natural world. Engineers use physics to build bridges, design electrical circuits, and develop computer games.

Dr. Duilia De Mello is an astrophysicist. She uses physics and astronomy to find out how our galaxy, the Milky Way, got its spiral shape.

Map of the Milky Way

Physicist Brian Cox gets paid to smash things! He uses special machines to smash atoms into each other. This helps scientists understand the structure of the universe.

iF YOU WANT TO DO COOL SCiENCE, KEEP ASKiNG QUESTiONS!

Jobs in Physical Science

Electrical Engineer
(electrical circuits)

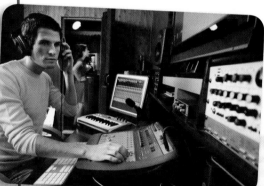

Sound Engineer
(sound, electrical circuits)

Civil Engineer
(force, motion)

Robotics Engineer
(force, motion)

Understanding Science Words

Understanding Special Terms

A science word becomes easier to understand when you break the word down into its different parts. Find out what each word part means, and you can figure out an unfamiliar science word.

Many science word parts come from the ancient languages of Latin and Greek.

Let's put two word parts together:

micro + scope = microscope

very small   *examine*   (an instrument that *examines very small* objects)

tech·nol·o·gy (těk
science, esp. to indu
tific method and m
...objective. 2. E

bio-

from Greek

means life

biology

-ology

from Greek

means field
of study

geology

photo-

from Greek

means light

photosynthesis

sol-

from Latin

means sun

solar

On the pages that
follow is a glossary of
the terms that are used
throughout this book.

-ist

from Greek, Latin

means one who
specializes in

geologist

Glossary

A

absorption taking in something, such as nutrients or light waves (246)

amber hardened tree resin (153)

amphibian an animal that spends part of its life cycle in water and the other part on land (66, 120)

anemometer a tool that measures wind direction and wind speed (191)

animal a living thing that moves, can reproduce by laying eggs or giving birth, and eats plants or other animals (64)

asteroid a chunk of rock that orbits the Sun (173)

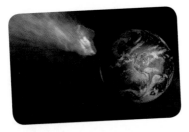

atmosphere the blanket of gases that surrounds Earth (171)

atom the smallest part of all matter (212)

axis an imaginary line that a planet spins around; runs through Earth from the North Pole to the South Pole (48, 260)

B

bacteria tiny organisms with just one cell (57, 165)

bar graph a graph that helps to compare data quickly (28)

behavior how an animal acts (62, 74)

biotechnology the science of using living things to help people (39)

bird an animal that has feathers, wings, two legs, a beak, and lays eggs with hard shells (67)

brain the organ in the nervous system that controls everything in your body (82)

buoyancy a force in the water that pushes up, keeping an object from sinking and causing it to float (255)

calorie a measure of the energy in food (89)

carbohydrate a nutrient in food that gives you energy (90)

cast fossil a type of fossil that was made when a mold fossil was filled with minerals that hardened over time (153)

cell the smallest part of a living thing (57)

change of state a physical change in which matter changes from one state to another: melting, condensing, vaporizing, or freezing (217)

chlorophyll the part of a plant that gives the plant its green color; captures energy from sunlight for photosynthesis (98)

chrysalis the stage in metamorphosis just before a caterpillar turns into a butterfly (119)

circulatory system the group of organs that helps blood get to all parts of your body (81)

cirrus cloud a thin, wispy cloud that forms on a pleasant day (196)

clay particles of soil that are very dense and close together (163)

climate the type of weather a place has over a long period of time (62, 197)

cloud a large cluster of very tiny drops of water in the sky (196)

coal a fossil fuel that is burned to make electricity (201, 226)

cold front a mass of cold air that replaces warmer air; brings strong thunderstorms and cooler weather (189)

color spectrum what is made when white light is separated into the colors red, orange, yellow, green, blue, indigo, and violet (247)

comet a chunk of dust and ice that travels in the solar system (173)

community a group of many populations that live in the same area (122)

compass a special tool that uses magnetism to show which way is north (261)

compost a mixture of decaying matter, such as dead leaves and twigs, that helps bring nutrients to the soil (167)

compound machine a machine that is made up of two or more simple machines (273)

conceptual model a model that is an educated guess (52)

condensing a change of state of matter from a gas to a liquid (217)

cone a part of some nonflowering plants which holds the seeds (105)

conservation ways to protect our natural resources (141)

core the inside layer of Earth (148)

crust the outer layer of Earth (148)

cumulonimbus cloud a rain cloud (196)

cumulus cloud a fluffy white cloud that indicates fair weather (196)

 D

data science information (22, 26)

day the time it takes for Earth to make one full rotation on its axis; 24 hours (46)

deciduous describes trees that lose their leaves in the fall (126)

desert an ecosystem that is very hot and dry and does not receive much rain (124)

digestive system the group of organs that breaks down food and gets rid of the things your body doesn't need (81, 86)

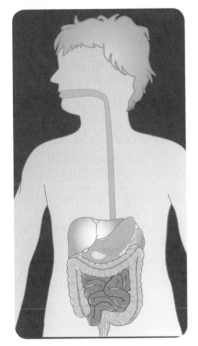

◉ E

earthquake shaking of the ground caused by a release of energy deep below Earth's surface (138)

echo a sound created when sound waves hit a solid surface and bounce back to you (235)

echolocation the process of using echoes to help an animal "see" in the dark (235)

ecosystem a natural system in which living and nonliving things work together in a certain area (45, 122)

egg cell a special cell in organisms that can make a new organism (104)

ellipse shaped like an oval, the type of orbit the planets have (170)

endangered species organisms that might become extinct (77, 131)

English system of measurement the system of measurement used most in daily life (284)

energy what makes things move or change (201, 220)

environment an area that is made up of living and nonliving things (58)

Equator the imaginary line that divides the Northern Hemisphere and the Southern Hemisphere (197)

erosion a change caused by wind and moving water that wears down Earth's surface (136, 158, 204)

esophagus a long tube in the digestive system that pushes food into the stomach (87)

experiment in science, a test (20)

extinct describes an organism that does not live or grow anywhere (76, 131)

 F

fat a nutrient in food that can be used for energy (90)

fish an animal that has fins and uses gills to breathe underwater (66)

flower the part of a plant that holds the seeds (100)

fog a cloud that has formed close to the ground (189)

food chain a path that shows how organisms get their food (128, 224)

Food Pyramid a guide to help us make good food choices (92)

force a push or a pull (223, 250, 256)

fossil the remains, in stone, of a living thing that died a long time ago (152)

fossil fuel a fuel formed from animals and plants that died a very long time ago (199, 226)

freezing a change of state of matter from a liquid to a solid (217)

friction a force that causes moving things to slow down or stop (254)

fulcrum the stable object or point on which a lever turns (266)

full moon a phase of the Moon in which we can see one whole side of the Moon (49)

fungi tiny organisms that help bacteria break down dead matter in soil (166)

 G

gas a state of matter that does not have shape or volume (216)

geologist a person who studies the rocks and minerals of Earth (40, 149)

germinate in plants, to sprout or grow (101)

gills body parts that help an animal breathe in water (63, 66, 121)

glacier a mass of ice that started out as snow and changed to ice (137)

glucose a sugar that plants make when they use energy from the Sun (99)

graduated cylinder a science tool that is used to measure the volume of liquids (36)

grassland an ecosystem where most of the plants are grasses (127)

gravel soil made up of small pieces of rocks (143)

gravity a force that pulls objects toward each other and toward the center of Earth (109, 174, 223, 252)

 H

habitat a place where an animal lives and gets all of the things it needs (70, 123)

hand lens a science tool that makes it easier to see small things (36)

heart the organ in the circulatory system that pumps blood throughout your body (82)

heart muscle muscle that makes your heart beat automatically (84)

heat energy energy made from moving atoms (227, 240)

hibernate, hibernation a state of deep rest that lets an animal survive the winter without food (75, 195)

hill a small mound of land (134)

humus found in the topsoil; contains dead leaves and twigs (150)

hurricane a huge storm, with strong winds and rain, that forms over warm ocean water (193)

 I

igneous rock rock that has melted, cooled, and hardened (147, 204)

inclined plane a tilted surface, like a ramp; is used to go up or down (270)

inherit when offspring receives characteristics from parents (61)

insect an invertebrate that has six legs and one or two pairs of wings (69)

invertebrate an animal without a backbone (68)

 J

joint the place where two bones come together (83)

K

kinetic energy energy that is in motion (222)

 L

landform a feature that exists on Earth's surface; includes mountains, hills, valleys, plains, and plateaus (134)

large intestine an organ in the digestive system that takes in water from undigested food (87)

larva the stage in metamorphosis that is hatched from an egg (118)

lava magma that flows out to Earth's surface (139, 147, 204)

leaf, leaves the part of a plant that makes a plant's food (100)

lever a long bar or board that turns on a pivot point called a fulcrum (266)

life cycle all of the changes a living thing goes through from birth to death (110)

life span the amount of time between birth and death (113)

light a form of energy that moves in waves (238)

light energy a form of energy from the Sun (240)

lightning an electric current caused by pieces of ice high up in the atmosphere (192)

line graph a graph that shows how data change over time (29)

liquid a state of matter that takes the shape of the container it is in (216)

lungs two organs that help an animal to breathe in and out on land (63, 82, 121)

luster the way the surface of a mineral reflects light (145)

M

magma melted rock from deep inside Earth's surface (139, 147, 204)

magnet an object that can pull or push things without touching them (256)

magnetic field the area that surrounds a magnet where the force of magnetism is felt (258)

magnetism a force that can pull or push things without touching them (256)

mammals animals that usually give birth to live young and have hair or fur (67)

mantle the middle layer of Earth (148)

map a drawing that shows where things are located (276)

mass a measure of how much matter there is in something (35, 37, 214, 253)

material resource anything we use and eat (200)

matter anything that takes up space (212)

mechanical energy the energy in matter; can be energy that is stored or energy that is moving (222)

melting a change of state of matter from a solid to a liquid (217)

metamorphic rock rock formed when pressure squeezes sedimentary and igneous rocks for a very long time (147, 204)

metamorphosis a process in which an animal changes shape as it grows into an adult (118)

meteorologist a person who uses technology to study the weather (40)

metric ruler, meterstick, measuring tape science tools that are used to measure length (37)

metric system the system of measurement that is often used for science projects (37, 284)

microscope a science tool that helps you see things that are too small to see with your eyes alone (36)

migration the movement of an animal from one place to another place in the winter (75, 195)

mineral a solid object that forms crystals; also a nutrient in food that helps our bodies build tissues (91, 142)

mixture a combination of two or more kinds of matter (218)

model a representation of what something looks like (50)

mold fossil a type of fossil in which an impression was left in soft sediment (153)

moon a natural object in space that orbits a planet (174, 176)

motion the movement of something from one place to another (222, 248)

mountain the tallest landform on Earth (134)

muscle an organ or a type of tissue that allows movement (84)

muscular system the group of organs that helps you move (81, 84)

 N

natural gas a fossil fuel that is burned to heat stoves and houses (201, 226)

natural resource something from Earth that we can use to make things we need or want (140, 198)

nervous system the group of organs that helps control your actions (81)

new moon a phase of the Moon in which we cannot see any part of it (49)

nonrenewable resource a natural resource that cannot be replaced (199)

North Pole (on Earth) the northernmost end of Earth's axis (260)

north pole (of a magnet) the end of a magnet that is attracted to the south pole of another magnet (260)

nutrients chemicals in food that help your body grow and stay healthy (90)

Nutrition Facts a label on packaged food that describes the nutrients and calories in the food (94)

Nutrition Facts
Serving Size 1 cup (228g)
Servings Per Container 2

Per Serving   Calories from Fat 110

Daily Value*

observation what you see, hear, touch, taste, or smell (18)

ocean an ecosystem that consists of a large body of salt water (124, 135)

oceanographer a person who studies the oceans (282)

offspring new organisms that come from the parents (61)

oil a fossil fuel that is used to make gasoline (226)

opaque describes an object that does not let light pass through it (243)

orbit the path of one object around another object (170)

organ a part of the body that does a special job (80)

organ system a group of organs that work together (80)

organism a living thing (56)

ovary the part of a plant where the seeds form (104)

paleontologist a person who studies prehistoric life (158)

pattern a set of items or events that is repeated (46, 189)

phase the shape of the bright part of the Moon; it changes over the course of a month (49, 175)

photosynthesis the process that plants use to make their own food (98)

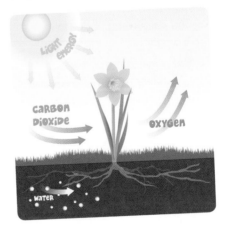

LIGHT ENERGY

CARBON DIOXIDE

OXYGEN

WATER

physical change a change in matter that does not change the type of matter that it is; for example, bending, mixing, or melting (215)

physical map a map that shows natural features, such as mountains, rivers, deserts, and lakes (277)

physical model a model that is a drawing or a diagram, or built out of wood, paper, clay, or other materials (52)

physical property a property that tells you something about matter without changing what the matter is (213)

pie graph a graph that compares parts of the whole (29)

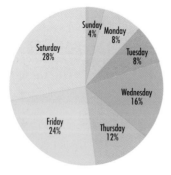

pitch how high or low a sound is (232)

plain a large, flat area of land that does not have many trees (134)

planet a natural body in the sky that moves around a star in an orbit (170)

plant an organism that can make its own food and reproduce (96)

plateau an area of flat land that is higher than the land around it (134)

political map a map that shows the borders around areas such as states or countries (277)

pollen a yellow powder on a plant that helps flowers make new plants (104)

pollination the part of a plant's life cycle when the plant makes seeds (104)

pollution what happens when something is released into the environment that can hurt living things and natural resources (206)

population a group of the same kind of living thing that lives in an area (122)

potential energy energy that is stored (222)

precipitation the weather word for any form of water (rain, snow, sleet, or hail) that falls to Earth from the sky (190)

predict to say what you think will happen (24)

protein a nutrient in food that helps build strong muscles (91)

protozoa tiny one-celled organisms that eat bacteria (165)

pulley a rope wrapped around one or more wheels which is used to lift an object up, down, or sideways (269)

 R

rain forest an ecosystem that is very warm and wet and found near Earth's equator (125)

rays straight lines of light (238)

recycle to reuse old materials in a new way (141, 207)

reflection the bouncing of light waves off an object and back to our eyes (242)

refraction the bending of light waves as they move from one kind of matter into another (244)

renewable resource a natural resource that does not run out (199)

reproduce, reproduction what organisms do to make more organisms like themselves (61, 112)

reptile an animal that has leathery skin and lays eggs with shells (66)

respiratory system the group of organs that helps you breathe (81)

rock a hard piece of Earth made of minerals (135, 142)

rock cycle a process in which one type of rock can change into a different type of rock (204)

root the part of a plant that holds the plant in the ground and takes in water and nutrients from the soil (100)

rotation the spin of Earth on its axis (48)

saliva a digestive juice in the mouth (86)

sand soil that is coarse and dry and made of tiny pieces or rock (143, 162)

satellite an object that orbits a planet; can be natural or made by people (179)

science notebook a place to write down important observations, questions, and answers about science (22)

scientific method the steps scientists use to find answers (19)

screw a long inclined plane wrapped around a rod; is used to hold things together (272)

season a period of the year that has a particular type of weather; spring, summer, fall, and winter (194)

sediment tiny pieces of rock, sand, and soil (152)

sedimentary rock rock formed from buried rocks that harden after they are pressed together over a long time (146, 204)

seed the part of a plant that holds the beginning of a new plant (101, 114)

seedling a young plant (114)

shadow what is made when an opaque object blocks light (245)

silt particles of soil that are gritty and very fine (162)

simple machine a simple tool that make work easier; e.g. a pulley, wedge, screw, inclined plane, and wheel and axle (264)

skeletal muscle muscle that is attached to bones (84)

skeletal system the group of organs that holds you up and protects the parts inside your body (81, 82)

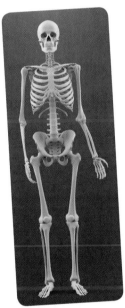

small intestine an organ in the digestive system that is connected to the stomach (87)

smooth muscle muscle that is found in the walls of some organs, such as the stomach (84)

soil a mixture of small pieces of rocks and living things (135, 150, 160)

solar system a group of planets and other objects that move around a star (44, 168)

solid a state of matter that keeps its shape, even when it is moved from one place to another (216)

sound a form of energy that is made when objects vibrate (228)

sound waves vibrations that form when an object moves back and forth very quickly (228)

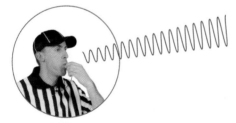

South Pole (on Earth) the southernmost end of Earth's axis (260)

south pole (of a magnet) the end of a magnet that is attracted to the north pole of another magnet (260)

speed how fast or slow something moves (249)

spinal cord a bundle of nerves that runs from the brain along the backbone (82)

spore what some nonflowering plants use to make new plants (105, 114)

stamen the part of a plant that makes pollen (104)

star a glowing object in the sky that is most visible at night (169)

state of matter one of three forms of matter: solid, liquid, or gas (216)

stem the part of a plant that supports the plant and helps water and nutrients get from the roots to the leaves (100)

stigma the sticky part of a plant where the pollen lands (104)

stomach an organ in the digestive system where food is mixed (87)

stopwatch a science tool that is used to measure time (37)

stratus cloud a low cloud that can produce light rain or mist (196)

streak the color a mineral makes when it is scraped on white tile (145)

Sun the star around which the planets in our solar system orbit (172)

system an organized group of parts that must work together to make a whole (42)

T

table a way to show data in an organized way (27)

tadpole the second stage in the life cycle of a frog or toad (121)

tally table a table with marks used to count things (26)

technology tools that help us solve problems (38)

temperature a measure of how hot or cold something is (36, 171, 190, 214, 287)

thematic map a map that shows information about a topic or a theme (277)

| Shortgrass | Mixed-grass | Tallgrass |

thermometer a tool that measures temperature (36, 190)

threatened species organisms whose population gets smaller and smaller (131)

thunderstorm a storm with heavy rain, lightning, thunder, strong winds, and sometimes hail (192)

tornado a funnel cloud that touches the ground during a storm (192)

trace fossil a fossil that tells us about an animal's behavior or environment; can be a footprint or a burrow (153)

translucent describes an object that lets a small amount of light pass through it (243)

transparent describes an object that lets most light pass through it (243)

tundra an ecosystem near the North Pole that is very cold but not covered in ice or snow (125)

two-pan balance, triple-beam balance science tools that are used to measure mass (37)

U

universe the largest system we know of; includes everything in space (45)

V

valley a narrow area of land (134)

vaporizing a change of the state of matter from a liquid to a gas (217)

vertebrate an animal with a backbone (66)

vibrate to move back and forth very quickly (228)

vitamin a nutrient in food that helps keep our bodies healthy (91)

vocal chords special folds inside your throat that make sound when air goes over them (233)

volcano a landform, or hole in Earth, from which magma erupts (138)

volume a measure of how much space something takes up; also how loud or quiet something is (35, 36, 214, 231, 286)

W

waning phases of the Moon when the bright part gets smaller (49)

warm front a mass of warm air that moves over colder air; usually produces light rain or fog (189)

water the most important nutrient for our bodies (91)

water cycle the process in which water is recycled over and over again from Earth's surface to the atmosphere and back again (173, 202)

waxing phases of the Moon when the bright part gets larger (49)

weather what the air is doing outside (186)

weather pattern weather that repeats over and over again (189)

weathering a process in which rocks are worn away by wind or rain (136, 160)

wedge a triangular object used to split things (271)

wheel and axle simple machine made of a small rod that goes through the center of a wheel; it allows you to move objects placed on the axle easily (268)

wind the movement of air (44, 191)

wind speed how fast the air is moving (191)

world map a map that shows all of Earth's continents and oceans (276)

Answer Key

Science Basics

ORGANIZING DATA

Science Notebook page **26**
There are 18 zebras in the field.

PATTERNS

Thinking BIG—SEM page **47**
A bee's eye

Life Science

ORGANISMS

What's in a School? page **56**
Your school environment has nonliving things, such as desks, chairs, paper, and pencils. Your school environment also has living things, such as all the students and teachers, and maybe even some animals.

An Animal Has to Eat! page **59**
3. Same: The teeth are white and hard.
4. Different: The teeth in Picture A are pointy and sharp. The teeth in Picture B are flatter.

5. B, cow

6. A, lion

7. It would have sharp teeth for tearing and flat teeth for grinding.

Thinking BIG—SEM paGe 63

A pill bug

Animals

Many Different Animals paGe 65

4. A heron flies; a tarantula walks; a butterfly flies; a prairie dog walks; a lion walks.

5. A heron has feathers; a tarantula has hair; a prairie dog has fur; a lion has fur.

6. Herons live near lakes; butterflies live in gardens; prairie dogs live underground; lions live in dens.

Thinking BIG—SEM paGe 68

One fish scale

What Do Animals Need? paGe 70

Animals need a habitat with food, water, space, and a place to live.

Backyard Safari paGe 71

1a. Maybe you live on a farm near some woods. The weather might be hot in summer and cold in winter.

1b. The nonliving things on the farm are soil and barns. The living things are dogs, cows, horses, plants, and trees.

2. Foxes live in this habitat.

3. This habitat will have small animals, such as mice, for the foxes to eat. The woods give the foxes a place to live.

4. When we study animals, we learn that human beings are similar animals. People and animals need food, water, and shelter.

HUMAN BODY

Your Amazing Body

1. Did you make your bed and get dressed? You probably brushed your teeth and ate breakfast. Then you walked to school.

2. You used your arms to make your bed and get dressed. You used your hand to brush your teeth. You used your hands and teeth to eat breakfast. You used your legs to walk to school.

3. Can you jump really far? Can you run fast or climb a wall? What else can you do?

Which Is Which?

brain: nervous system
stomach: digestive system
nose: respiratory system
heart: circulatory system
muscles: muscular system

Mighty Muscle!

1. Your biceps muscle feels soft. It is resting.

2. Your biceps muscle feels hard. It is shorter.

3. You can point your toes, smile, lift your leg, bend at the waist, and open and close your mouth.

FOOD ENERGY

What Are the Nutrients? PAGE 90

We need carbohydrates, fats, proteins, water, vitamins, and minerals.

Snack Attack! PAGE 95

2. Snack B

3. Snack B has fewer calories from fat. The foods in Snack B also come from different food groups.

PLANTS

Let the Sun Shine PAGE 99

6. The plant in the sunlight looks healthier. The plants need the Sun to grow.

7. The plant that does not get sunlight does not grow as well and will die.

8. Plants need sunlight in order to make their own food.

Which Way Is Up? PAGE 103

4. You'll see that the plant is starting to bend upward.

5. The plant is growing in the opposite direction from gravity.

Thinking BIG—SEM PAGE 105

A plant seed

Life Cycles

What Is the Life Cycle? page 110

The four parts of a life cycle are birth, becoming an adult, reproduction, and death.

Growing Up page 112

2. You were small and didn't have any hair. You also had very small fingers and toes.

3. You have teeth. You are taller and stronger and weigh more. You have lots of hair.

4. You could cry and laugh. You could roll over.

5. You can walk and run. You can talk and eat many things. You can ride a bike. You can read.

6. You will be able to reach taller things. You will be able to run faster and read harder books.

How Will It Grow? page 115

Maybe you found a maple tree "helicopter." Be sure to draw the four stages of the maple tree's life cycle.

Thinking BIG—SEM page 117

Inside an eggshell

Ecosystems

What Is a Habitat? page 123

Maybe your favorite animal is a cow. A cow lives on a farm and has hay and grass to eat and water to drink. The cow lives in a barn.

We're All in This Together page 127

1. a park community

2. A park community might include populations of birds, oak trees, maple trees, squirrels, and grass and other plants.

It All Depends page 129

1. You might live near a forest.

2. Plants in the forest include birch and oak trees.

3. Animals in a forest include deer, snakes, coyotes, birds, mice, and flies.

4. The deer eat the plants, and the coyotes eat the mice.

5. The birds need the trees to make their nests.

◎ Earth Science

Minerals and Rocks

Which Is Which? page 146

1. metamorphic

2. sedimentary

3. igneous

Rock Group page 147

You may notice many features. You may sort rocks by their size, by whether they are smooth or rough, by their color, by their weight, or by some other properties.

FOSSILS

What Becomes a Fossil?

Fossils can be made from the remains of animals and plants, and from footprints, burrows, and other things.

Then and Now

Fern leaves and fish have not changed much over time.

SOIL

How Does Your Garden Grow?

5. All of your seeds probably grew. The bean in gravel may have grown the fastest. It did not need much energy to push through the loose gravel. The bean in soil may have grown very fast. It had all the nutrients it needed. The bean in sand probably grew most slowly. The sand was too heavy for the plant to push through easily.

Which Is Which?

gritty: silt
slimy: clay
coarse and dry: sand

Thinking BIG—SEM

Sand

weather, seasons, and climate

Which Is Which? **PAGE 186**

You might wear a raincoat and rain boots on a rainy day. Snow boots, mittens, a hat, scarf, and a warm jacket are needed on a cold, snowy day. On a warm, sunny day, you might wear a short-sleeve shirt, shorts, and sandals.

Weather Watching **PAGE 187**

The weather in your area might be warm, cloudy, rainy, windy, snowy, sunny, or cold. There are many possibilities.

natural resources

Which Is Which? **PAGE 199**

Water is renewable; coal is nonrenewable; the Sun is renewable; wind is renewable.

Name That Material! **PAGE 200**

Your notebook may be one example. The notebook may have paper and metal rings. Paper is made from trees. Trees are renewable. Metal is made from minerals. Minerals are nonrenewable.

Drowning in Bottles **PAGE 207**

2. You can drink water from the tap or use a pitcher that filters water. You can buy juice in large containers.

⦿ Physical Science

MATTER

Will It Float? PAGE 213

1. A cork and a rubber stopper are each the same shape. They are both smooth. A cork is stiff. A rubber stopper bends. A toothpick and a birthday candle are both about the same length. The toothpick is thinner than the candle.

2. You may think that the cork, the candle, and the toothpick will float. The stopper will sink.

3. All of them floated.

4. It tell you that the cork, birthday candle, toothpick, and rubber stopper all have the same physical property of being able to float.

Fix the Mix PAGE 219

1. You would not use shape to separate the mixture. All of the objects are long and thin.

2. You could use a magnet to pull the nails out of the mixture. Nails are magnetic. Toothpicks and plastic are not magnetic.

3. You could use water to make the toothpicks float. The nails will not float. The plastic mixers will not float.

4. When you put the mixture in water, the toothpicks floated. You could use a magnet to separate the nails. You could use water to make the toothpicks float. The plastic mixers would be the only parts of the mixture left.

EnerGY

You Can't Beat Energy! paGe 221

1. When you hit the drum softly, it made a quiet sound. When you hit it harder, the sound was louder. The second sound was louder because you used more energy when you hit the drum.

2. When you hit the drumstick, it sounded like you were hitting the drum. The energy that you used to hit the drumstick moved through the drumstick and into the drum. The energy of your moving arm changed into sound energy coming from the drum.

Fun in the Sun! paGe 225

5. You may think thermometers 2 and 3 will be the same temperature, but 2 will become hotter.

6. Every investigation will be different. For example, you may find that thermometer 1 shows 85°F, thermometer 2 shows 89°F, and thermometer 3 shows 83°F. The temperatures will be different.

7. More heat will reach the thermometer under the black cloth. Less heat will reach the thermometer under the white cloth.

SOUND

Listen Up! Page 229

2. Can you hear the hum of a heater? Maybe you can hear birds outside.

4. A nearby sound does not need as much energy to reach your ears. A sound from far away needs more energy because it has to travel farther.

Let's Hear It for Sound! Page 231

1. When you clapped as loud as possible, your hands probably stung a little.

2. When you clapped softly, you only felt your hands touching.

3. When you clapped loudly, you used more energy. The force of your hands hitting each other was greater. Making a loud sound used more energy and created a stronger force than making a soft sound.

Is It High or Low? Page 232

For example, a bird makes a high-pitched sound. A cow makes a low-pitched sound.

Musical Glasses Page 233

3. The glass with the most water had the highest pitch. The glass with no water had the lowest pitch.

4. The pitch changes because there isn't much air space in the full glass of water, so the sound waves move quickly in the small amount of space. When there is a lot of air space, the sound waves move more slowly. The pitch is lower.

LiGHT

Where Do We Get Light?
light bulbs, Sun, fireflies, flashlight, lamps, matches, candles

Light Coming Through!
3. If you looked through a piece of paper, you might be able to see through it a little. If you chose a book, you found that you could not see through it because it is opaque. Hold up a drinking glass, and you'll find that you can see completely through it. Clear glass is transparent.

Refraction Magic
4. Before water was added, you couldn't see the coin because the rim blocked the light waves from reaching your eye. When water was added to the bowl, the light waves bent because of refraction. The light waves bent just enough to miss the rim of the bowl, and then you could see the coin.

Get the Message
3. Each color of cellophane absorbed light waves of the same color. Using red, yellow, and green together allowed only blue light waves to reflect off the paper. Then you could see the message.

MOTION AND FORCES

On the Move!

2. Your examples may be a bird, a car, and a swing. A bird flew straight. Car wheels moved in a circle. A swing moved back and forth.

3. The bird also moved up and down. The car wheels also moved forward. The swing moved up and down.

4. Nothing moved at exactly the same speed as other things moved.

Pull or Push?

The snowplow is pushing snow. The horse is pulling the sleigh. The woman is pushing the swing. The boy is pulling the leaves.

What's the Word? 251

2. Train: Type of Motion: straight, but sometimes curved; Speed: very fast; Amount of Force: a lot.
Falling snow: Type of Motion: down; Speed: slow; Amount of Force: not much.
Swing: Type of Motion: back and forth; Speed: fast; Amount of Force: some.

Hang On! 253

4. The more marbles you added, the heavier the carton became. Gravity pulled down the marbles and made the rubber band stretch.

Magnetism

A Magnetic Investigation PAGE 256

2. You may predict that all of the metal objects will be pulled by the magnet.

4. You may be surprised. Some metals, like a nickel coin, will not be pulled by the magnet. The coin contains metal that is not attracted to magnets. When the magnet pulls, you know the object has metal in it that is attracted to a magnet.

Which End Is Which? PAGE 257

4. You may predict that if the marked ends of both magnets are Xs, then the unmarked ends are both circles. They will repel each other. If the marked end of the bar magnet has a circle and the horseshoe magnet has an X, then the unmarked ends will also attract each other.

Magnetism Coming Through! PAGE 259

3. The magnet pulled the paper clip toward the side of most of the containers. This means the magnetic field went through the materials.

4. The paper clip did not move when it was inside a wide container. The magnetic field was too weak to reach the middle of the wide containers.

Make Your Point! PAGE 261

3. The needle points north. When you turn the dish, the needle keeps pointing in the same direction.

Match Play PaGe 263

1. c

2. a

3. d

4. b

SimPLe MaCHiNes

Find the Machine PaGe 265

4. You might have found these simple machines: wheel and axle: doorknob, used to open a door; pulley: window blinds, used to open and shut blinds; wedge: pushpins, used to hold papers on bulletin boards; lever: bottle opener, used to open bottles; screw: jar lid, used to open and close jars; inclined plane: slide, used to get from the top to the bottom

Can I Get a Lift? PaGe 267

2. You probably couldn't lift the brick when the fulcrum was close to the end where you were pushing.

3. You could lift the brick when the fulcrum was in the middle.

4. The brick was easiest to lift when the fulcrum was close to the brick.

Which Is Which? PaGe 272

1. lever

2. wedge

3. pulley

Reading Maps

Parts of a Map

page 279

B4; the Visitor Center

Picture Credits

Characters Marcin Wierzchowski, www.hmmmstudio.pl; **Graphic Novels** Mark Sugar; **Cover** 1a ©iStockphoto.com/zbindere; 1b ©iStockphoto.com/lightpix; **Science Basics** 18a ©iStockphoto.com/AndreasReh; 18b NASA/Courtesy of nasaimages. org; 18c ©iStockphoto.com/joeygil; 18d ©iStockphoto.com/jophil; 19a Donovan Foote; 21a Donovan Foote; 23a ©iStockphoto.com/rusm; 24a ©iStockphoto.com/bonniej; 24b ©iStockphoto.com/rusm; 24c Donovan Foote; 25a ©iStockphoto.com/rusm; 25b ©iStockphoto.com/Alina555; 26a ©iStockphoto.com/GlobalP; 26b ©iStockphoto.com/ kozmoat98; 26c ©iStockphoto.com/belterz; 27a ©iStockphoto.com/photosfromafrica; 27b ©iStockphoto.com/GP232; 27c ©iStockphoto.com/ottokalman; 29a ©iStockphoto.com/rainbow-7; 29b ©iStockphoto.com/ewenjc; 30a ©iStockphoto.com/yucelyilmaz; 30b ©iStockphoto.com/stray cat; 30c ©iStockphoto.com/foxtalbot; 31a Donovan Foote; 31b ©iStockphoto.com/morganl; 31c Donovan Foote; 31d ©iStockphoto.com/Funwithfood; 32a-c Donovan Foote; 33a-c Carolina Biological Supply Company; 33d ©iStockphoto.com/EyeJoy; 34a ©iStockphoto.com/kvkirillov; 34b ©iStockphoto.com/AndersSellin; 34c ©iStockphoto.com/Maica; 35a ©iStockphoto.com/claylib; 35b ©iStockphoto.com/ LongHa2006; 36a ©iStockphoto.com/stray_cat; 36b ©iStockphoto.com/claylib; 36c ©iStockphoto.com/JBryson; 37a ©iStockphoto.com/sak12344; 37b ©iStockphoto.com/marcusarm; 37c Carolina Biological Supply Company; 37d Carolina Biological Supply Company; 38a ©iStockphoto.com/nicoolay; 38b ©iStockphoto.com/wpohldesign; 38c U.S. Army; 38d ©iStockphoto.com/nano; 39a ©iStockphoto.com/PhotoEuphoria; 39b ©iStockphoto.com/Creativeye99; 39c ©iStockphoto.com/DenGuy; 40a ©iStockphoto.com/ChuckSchugPhotography; 40a NASA/Courtesy of nasaimages.org; 40b ©iStockphoto.com/cristimatei; 40b-c Donovan Foote; 41a ©iStockphoto.com/gchutka; 41b ©iStockphoto.com/ MichaelSvoboda; 41c NASA/Courtesy of nasaimages.org; 41d ©iStockphoto.com/PhotoEuphoria; 42a ©iStockphoto.com/ amysuem; 42b ©iStockphoto.com/Jimak; 42c ©iStockphoto.com/RBFried; 43a ©iStockphoto.com/ttbphoto; 43b ©iStockphoto.com/DaydreamsGirl; 44a ©iStockphoto.com/appleuzr; 44b ©iStockphoto.com/rcp; 46a ©iStockphoto.com/ bobbieo; 46b ©iStockphoto.com/zxcynosure; 46c ©iStockphoto.com/Kasiam; 46d ©iStockphoto.com/margo-rita; 46e ©iStockphoto.com/intransfer; 46f ©iStockphoto.com/Lezh; 47a ©iStockphoto.com/DNY59; 47b ©iStockphoto.com/ bjenkin; 47c ©iStockphoto.com/borchee; 47d ©iStockphoto.com/Snowleopard1; 47e Carolina Biological Supply Company; 48a ©iStockphoto.com/pictureland; 48b ©iStockphoto.com/tombonatti; 48c ©iStockphoto.com/evirgen; 50a ©iStockphoto.com/AlesVeluscek; 51b ©iStockphoto.com/Eraxion; 52a ©iStockphoto.com/webking; 52b ©iStockphoto.com/Brosa; 52c ©iStockphoto.com/kryczka; 53a ©iStockphoto.com/ManoAfrica; **Organisms** 56a ©iStockphoto.com/skynesher; 57a ©iStockphoto.com/clearviewstock; 57b ©iStockphoto.com/Eraxion; 57c-d Carolina Biological Supply Company; 57e ©iStockphoto.com/CathyKeifer; 57f ©iStockphoto.com/photo75; 58a ©iStockphoto.com/ diademimages; 58b ©iStockphoto.com/FourOaks; 59a ©iStockphoto.com/SHOPTOOMUCH; 59b ©iStockphoto.com/ johan63; 59c ©iStockphoto.com/candyfloss; 60a ©iStockphoto.com/HKPNC; 60b ©iStockphoto.com/GlobalP; 60c ©iStockphoto.com/mchen007; 60d ©iStockphoto.com/pontific; 61a ©iStockphoto.com/Slonov; 61b ©iStockphoto.com/ colevineyard; 61c ©iStockphoto.com/pjmalsbury; 62a ©iStockphoto.com/DmitryND; 62b ©iStockphoto.com/Andrew_ Howe; 62c ©iStockphoto.com/cherokeejones; 63a ©iStockphoto.com/DmitryND; 63b ©iStockphoto.com/rusm; 63c ©iStockphoto.com/HTuller; 63d Carolina Biological Supply Company; **Animals** 64a-d Carolina Biological Supply Company; 65a Carolina Biological Supply Company; 67a ©iStockphoto.com/mykidsmom; 67b ©iStockphoto.com/doucettej; 67c ©iStockphoto.com/irvingnsaperstein; 68a ©iStockphoto.com/AlasdairJames; 68a ©iStockphoto.com/GlobalP; 68b Carolina Biological Supply Company; 68b ©iStockphoto.com/Captainflash; 68c ©iStockphoto.com/tomonikon; 68d Carolina Biological Supply Company; 69a ©iStockphoto.com/davidnavratil; 69b-d Carolina Biological Supply Company; 70a ©iStockphoto.com/JoeGough; 70b ©iStockphoto.com/ChuckSchugPhotography; 70b ©iStockphoto.com/NNehring; 70d ©iStockphoto.com/gioadventures; 70e ©iStockphoto.com/tirc83; 70f ©iStockphoto.com/milehightraveler; 71a ©iStockphoto.com/ktsimage; 71b ©iStockphoto.com/emreogan; 74a ©iStockphoto.com/Antagain; 74b ©iStockphoto.com/bbszabi; 74c ©iStockphoto.com/kawisign; 75a ©iStockphoto.com/LyaC; 75b ©iStockphoto.com/ Gordo25; 75c Kristen Naffah; 76a ©iStockphoto.com/OlgaBel; 76b Carolina Biological Supply Company; 77a ©iStockphoto.com/alexsl; 77b ©iStockphoto.com/Taso_H; 77c ©iStockphoto.com/GlobalP; **The Human Body** 78a ©iStockphoto.com/bonniej; 78b ©iStockphoto.com/goldenangel; 78c ©iStockphoto.com/huaxiadragon; 79a ©iStockphoto.com/Juanmonino; 79b ©iStockphoto.com/barsik; 80a ©iStockphoto.com/lucato; 80b Donovan Foote; 80c ©iStockphoto.com/kwanisik; 82a ©iStockphoto.com/avajjon; 82b ©iStockphoto.com/imagestock; 83a ©iStockphoto.com/ infospeed; 83b ©iStockphoto.com/kkgas; 83c ©iStockphoto.com/Spauln; 83d ©iStockphoto.com/narawon; 84a ©iStockphoto.com/sjlocke; 84b-d Carolina Biological Supply Company; 85a ©iStockphoto.com/WillSelarep; 85b ©iStockphoto.com/McIninch; 85c ©iStockphoto.com/bj_digital; 86a ©iStockphoto.com/PacoRomero; 86b ©iStockphoto.com/wrangel; 87a Donovan Foote; **Food Energy** 88a ©iStockphoto.com/Dom15; 88b ©iStockphoto.com/

©iStockphoto.com/Liliboas; 164a Carolina Biological Supply Company; 165a ©iStockphoto.com/claylib; 165b ©iStockphoto.com/NNehring; 166a ©iStockphoto.com/busypix; 166b ©iStockphoto.com/arlindo71; 166c ©iStockphoto.com/clearviewstock; 167a ©iStockphoto.com/cjp; **Solar System** 168a ©iStockphoto.com/appleuzr; 169a ©iStockphoto.com/danmitchell; 169b ©iStockphoto.com/oorka; 169c NASA/Courtesy of nasaimages.org; 170a NASA/Courtesy of nasaimages.org; 171a Donovan Foote; 171b ©iStockphoto.com/janrysavy; 172a ©iStockphoto.com/JulyVelchev; 172b ©iStockphoto.com/Raycat; 172c Donovan Foote; 173a ©iStockphoto.com/BenGoode; 173b ©iStockphoto.com/magaliB; 173c portrait by Justus Sustermans; 174a Accurate Art; 174b ©iStockphoto.com/AndreyTTL; 175a ©iStockphoto.com/fanelliphotography; 175b Donovan Foote; 176a-c NASA/Courtesy of nasaimages.org; 177a NASA/Courtesy of nasaimages.org; **Space Exploration** 178a ©iStockphoto.com/Petrovich9; 178b ©iStockphoto.com/inhauscreative; 179a ©iStockphoto.com/TerryHealy; 179b ©iStockphoto.com/cristimatei; 180a ©iStockphoto.com/peterspiro; 180b ©iStockphoto.com/mrtom-uk; 180c NASA/Courtesy of nasaimages.org; 181a ©iStockphoto.com/parameter; 181b ©iStockphoto.com/Redemption; 182a ©iStockphoto.com/Daneel; 182b ©iStockphoto.com/RFStock; 183a NASA/Courtesy of nasaimages.org; 183b ©iStockphoto.com/Snaprender; 184a ©iStockphoto.com/Pgiam; 184b ©iStockphoto.com/Talshiar; 184c ©iStockphoto.com/ranplett; 185a NASA/Courtesy of nasaimages.org; **Weather, Seasons, and Climate** 186a ©iStockphoto.com/stevecoleccs; 186b ©iStockphoto.com/ManuelH; 186c ©iStockphoto.com/jtyler; 189a ©iStockphoto.com/DepthofField; 189b ©iStockphoto.com/BRANDONJ74; 189c-d Donovan Foote; 190a ©iStockphoto.com/eb75; 190b ©iStockphoto.com/DelmotteVivian; 191a Donovan Foote; 191b ©iStockphoto.com/Andyworks; 191c ©iStockphoto.com/arturoli; 192a ©iStockphoto.com/red_moon_rise; 192b ©iStockphoto.com/clintspencer; 193a ©iStockphoto.com/donald_gruener; 194a ©iStockphoto.com/Art-Y; 194b ©iStockphoto.com/mikedabell; 194c ©iStockphoto.com/rossario; 194d ©iStockphoto.com/LindaYolanda; 194e ©iStockphoto.com/JillLang; 195a ©iStockphoto.com/wweagle; 195c ©iStockphoto.com/Blair_witch; 195d ©iStockphoto.com/akaplummer; 195e ©iStockphoto.com/lightstalker; 196a ©iStockphoto.com/patrickoberem; 196b ©iStockphoto.com/ballycroy; 196c ©iStockphoto.com/Saturated; 196d ©iStockphoto.com/YinYang; 197a ©iStockphoto.com/heimphoto; **Natural Resources** 198a ©iStockphoto.com/fotoVoyager; 198b ©iStockphoto.com/kodachrome25; 198c ©iStockphoto.com/halfshag; 199a ©iStockphoto.com/acilo; 199b ©iStockphoto.com/globestock; 199c ©iStockphoto.com/vlynder; 200a ©iStockphoto.com/DNY59; 200b ©iStockphoto.com/cveltri; 200c ©iStockphoto.com/garymilner; 201a ©iStockphoto.com/Dutchy; 201b ©iStockphoto.com/brainstorm1962; 202a ©iStockphoto.com/jeremkin; 204a Donovan Foote; 205a ©iStockphoto.com/IlonaBudzbon; 205b ©iStockphoto.com/photoBeard; 205c ©iStockphoto.com/PetePattavina; 205d ©iStockphoto.com/ArtisticCaptures; 205e ©iStockphoto.com/tbradford; 205f ©iStockphoto.com/SKashkin; 206a ©iStockphoto.com/Kiyyah; 206b ©iStockphoto.com/milehightraveler; 206c ©iStockphoto.com/narvikk; 206d ©iStockphoto.com/steinphoto; 207a ©iStockphoto.com/LyaC; 208a ©iStockphoto.com/pryzmat; 209a ©iStockphoto.com/urbancow; **Matter** 212a ©iStockphoto.com/blueflames; 212b ©iStockphoto.com/OGphoto; 213a ©iStockphoto.com/IMPALASTOCK; 213b ©iStockphoto.com/DamianPalus; 214a ©iStockphoto.com/WitR; 214b ©iStockphoto.com/morganl; 214c ©iStockphoto.com/gethinlane; 215a ©iStockphoto.com/tmlgt; 215b ©iStockphoto.com/speyeder; 215c ©iStockphoto.com/muratsen; 216a Elissa Chamberlain; 216b ©iStockphoto.com/AdamG1975; 216c ©iStockphoto.com/jorgeantonio; 216d-e Elissa Chamberlain 216f ©iStockphoto.com/arakonyunus; 216g ©iStockphoto.com/stevenallan; 217a-b ©iStockphoto.com/eb75; 217c ©iStockphoto.com/AlesVeluscek; 217d ©iStockphoto.com/JulienGrondin; 217e ©iStockphoto.com/jrroman; 218a ©iStockphoto.com/QUAYSIDE; 218a ©iStockphoto.com/robynmac; 219b ©iStockphoto.com/DonNichols; 219c ©iStockphoto.com/jgroup; 219d ©iStockphoto.com/luismmolina; **Energy** 220a ©iStockphoto.com/contrails; 220b ©iStockphoto.com/track5; 220c ©iStockphoto.com/bjones27; 220d ©iStockphoto.com/ktphotog; 220e ©iStockphoto.com/AZ68; 221a ©iStockphoto.com/photosmash; 221b ©iStockphoto.com/mikdam; 222a ©iStockphoto.com/ajphoto; 222b ©iStockphoto.com/ChuckSchugPhotography; 222c ©iStockphoto.com/Sportstock; 222d ©iStockphoto.com/monkeybusinessimages; 222e ©iStockphoto.com/JanBer405; 222f ©iStockphoto.com/jml5571; 223a ©iStockphoto.com/farbenrausch; 223b ©iStockphoto.com/caracterdesign; 223c ©iStockphoto.com/KarenMower; 224a Accurate Art; 225a ©iStockphoto.com/stevenallan; 225b Donovan Foote; 226a ©iStockphoto.com/StonePhotos; 226b ©iStockphoto.com/skodonnell; 226c ©iStockphoto.com/AlexAvich; 227a ©iStockphoto.com/MaximShebeko; 227b ©iStockphoto.com/Mlenny; 227c ©iStockphoto.com/DJClaassen; **Sound** 228a ©iStockphoto.com/ManoAfrica; 228b ©iStockphoto.com/marses; 228c ©iStockphoto.com/mkm3; 229a ©iStockphoto.com/Cimmerian; 229b ©iStockphoto.com/kickers; 229c ©iStockphoto.com/gmattrichard; 229d Petr Kratochvil; 229e ©iStockphoto.com/paulaphoto; 230a ©iStockphoto.com/graphixel; 230b Donovan Foote; 231a ©iStockphoto.com/yingxiaoming; 231b ©iStockphoto.com/BryanLever; 231c ©iStockphoto.com/valdore; 232a ©iStockphoto.com/seahorse8080; 232b ©iStockphoto.com/zeljica; 232c ©iStockphoto.com/dstephens; 232d ©iStockphoto.com/spxChrome; 233a ©iStockphoto.com/ranplett; 233b ©iStockphoto.com/Matejay; 234a ©iStockphoto.com/akurtz; 234b ©iStockphoto.com/sbayram; 234c ©iStockphoto.com/sbayram; 234d ©iStockphoto.com/kenglye; 235a ©iStockphoto.com/art explosion; 236a ©iStockphoto.com/kkgas; 236b ©iStockphoto.com/christophriddle; 236c ©iStockphoto.com/KateLeigh; 237a ©iStockphoto.com/nico_blue; 237b ©iStockphoto.com/Larry_St_Pierre; 237c Courtesy of the United States Library of Congress; **Light** 238a ©iStockphoto.com/SchulteProductions; 238b ©iStockphoto.com/A-G-N-I; 238c ©iStockphoto.com/suc; 238d Donovan Foote; 239a Donovan Foote; 239b ©iStockphoto.com/SteveStone; 239c ©iStockphoto.com/AnikaSalsera; 240a

Index